/ 8 -55

BIBLIO=
THERAPY

Methods
and Materials

Committee on Bibliotherapy

MILDRED T. MOODY, Chairman

and

Subcommittee on the Troubled Child

HILDA K. LIMPER, Chairman

ASSOCIATION
OF HOSPITAL AND INSTITUTION LIBRARIES

AMERICAN LIBRARY ASSOCIATION
Chicago

International Standard Book Number 0-8389-3107-3 (1971)

Library of Congress Catalog Card Number 75-165199

Copyright © 1971 by the American Library Association

Printed in the United States of America

Second Printing, September 1973

Contents

Preface

In the past decade a number of things have happened to stimulate the production of this volume. The members of the Association of Hospital and Institution Libraries, since the beginning of the organization, have had a sustained interest in the therapeutic aspects of their branch of library service. This interest took concrete form in 1962 when Miss Ruth Tews, as chairman of the Bibliotherapy Committee, edited an issue of *Library Trends* devoted to the subject. This was followed two years later by a noteworthy interdisciplinary workshop on bibliotherapy at the ALA Conference in Saint Louis.

Following the workshop the Subcommittee on the Troubled Child was formed under the chairmanship of Miss Hilda Limper. Its purpose was to examine the field of children's literature to determine which titles would be helpful to children and adolescents with emotional and behavior problems. This committee's work resulted in nine annotated lists, which form Part 2 of this volume.

Another factor prompting publication of this book was the passage of Title IV-A and IV-B of the Library Services and Construction Act. With money available for upgrading state institution libraries and expanding service to the physically handicapped, more serious consideration was given to the library's role in therapeutic service to patients and inmates.

There is now a vast body of knowledge concerning education, the social sciences, and psychology which is applicable to the work of their ancillary professions. In the library this knowledge affects reader guidance and library group activities, and influences the selection of materials. Since formal training which would prepare the librarian to develop therapeutic library services is unavailable, present-day philosophies and practices are the outgrowth of in-service training, institutes, and workshops which have crossed many interdisciplinary lines.

It is from this background that the concept of therapeutic library service has grown. In the past one school of thought has considered this synonymous with a broad definition of the term "bibliotherapy." However, in the traditional context bibliotherapy is thought of as a controlled psychotherapeutic technique which may be used in individual guidance or for group discussions. In any event, the library's role in the therapeutic community—the institution—favors a broad definition. For institutional library service is guided by the same principles which govern the ancillary therapies, and is judged by whether or not it improves the level of patient or inmate care.

This handbook has two purposes. First, it presents a foundation for executing a therapeutic program based on current knowledge of the process of therapy, and suggests methods and materials; second, it lists books useful for young people facing difficulties in adjustment. It is hoped that the book will be useful to institutions in the development of meaningful library services, to librarians and therapists in using the resources of the library, and to students in library schools who may wish to learn about or choose a career in this rewarding area of service. The committees, having laid the groundwork, particularly hope that this volume will lead to serious research into the therapeutic value of reading.

In Part 1 the Bibliotherapy Committee has examined the broad aspects of the subject as they relate to the manifold problems confronting the person who finds himself in a hospital or institution. In Part 2 the Troubled Child Subcommittee has chosen explicit problem areas and selected specific titles which it hopes will be helpful to those who guide and counsel children with these maladjustments.

Special thanks are due Miss Eleanor Phinney, former executive secretary of AHIL, for her expertise in opening doors to publication and for serving in an advisory capacity to the committees; special thanks also are due Clara J. Kircher, a member of the committee, for her valuable editorial assistance in the preparation of Parts 1 and 2. Thanks are due also to the AHIL Board of Directors for their encouragement and final approval of the manuscript for publication; to the members of the Bibliotherapy Committee: Margaret C. Hannigan, Margaret M. Kinney, Clara J. Kircher, Hilda K. Limper, and Mildred T. Moody, chairman; and to the members of the Troubled Child Subcommittee: Barbara Ambler, Marilee Foglesong, Margaret M. Kimmel, Clara J. Kircher, Jane Manthorne, Doris Stotz, and Hilda K. Limper, chairman. Miss Limper prepared the author-title index for the list of books for the troubled child and the adolescent in Part 2.

PART II

Reading

as

Therapy

Prepared by the COMMITTEE ON BIBLIOTHERAPY
 Margaret C. Hannigan
 Margaret M. Kinney
 Clara J. Kircher
 Hilda K. Limper
 Mildred T. Moody, Chairman

Book discussion group,
Louisiana Correctional and
Industrial School,
DeQuincy, Louisiana

Bibliotherapy
and
Its Background

It is possible to say that bibliotherapy began in ancient times, for writers in classical Greece were well aware of the therapeutic effects of reading. Aristotle, for instance, believed that literature as well as the other arts aroused emotions within a person which had healing effects. The library at Thebes bore the inscription, "The Healing Place of the Soul." A similar inscription, "The Medicine Chest for the Soul," is found in the medieval Abbey Library of St. Gall, in Switzerland.

There have been a number of historical reviews published which trace the development of hospital library service and the concept of bibliotherapy, including those by McDaniel,[1] Beatty,[2] and Tews.[3] This chapter will, therefore, confine itself to those occurrences which have marked progress toward present-day library services.

John Minson Galt II, of Williamsburg, Virginia, was the first American to publish a book on the therapeutic nature of library service. Very serious consideration was given to the kinds of material chosen for the mentally ill to read during the middle of the nineteenth century. Books of a religious nature and those which were strongly moralistic were recommended, although Galt expanded his selections to include books of a general nature which were interesting but not too demanding intellectually, unless the reader was in need of more technical or scholarly material. In his survey of American asylums, issued in 1840, he lays down some general rules governing patients' reading, book selection, and management of the library.[4] His detailed coverage of libraries in foreign and American institutions indicates the importance which was attached to these services even at that time.

Early in the twentieth century the first organized hospital libraries which were under the administration of a trained librarian came into being. These were at Massachusetts General Hospital, Boston, and at McLean Hospital, a private mental institution at Waverley, Massachusetts. In 1904, Miss Alice S. Tyler, secretary of the Iowa Library Commission, persuaded the state library commission to provide collections of material in the state institutions, and an institutional library supervisor was appointed. This was the start of organized library service to state institutions.

The American Library Association sponsored a highly successful program of library service to the armed forces in World War I, based to some extent on existing library practices in hospitals and institutions. Congress appropriated funds for the care of the disabled soldiers, and following the war the U.S. Veterans Bureau assumed the administration of veterans' hospitals and provided library service to them. Among librarians who made notable contributions were Sadie Peterson Delaney at the Veterans Administration Hospital of Tuskeegee, Alabama, and Elizabeth Pomeroy, who was noted for her study of the reading interests of 1,538 patients in 62 VA facilities.[5]

As supervisor of institution libraries in Minnesota, Perrie Jones planned and administered the first library school course of study for hospital librarians. This was at the University of Minnesota. She solicited the aid of several psychiatrists in planning therapy programs, among them Dr. Gordon R. Kamman, who actively promoted bibliotherapy within the medical profession. Miss Jones organized library sessions at the annual conferences of the American Hospital Association during the 1920s and 1930s. Papers presented at these sessions, including Miss Jones' detailed survey of hospital library service in Europe and the United States,[6] were reported in the transactions of the Association for those years.

The American Library Association began its active support of hospital and institution libraries early in the twentieth century. It should be noted that the first textbook on hospital library service, *The Hospital Library* by E. Kathleen Jones,[7] was published by the Association in 1923. A short history of the Association of Hospital and Institution Libraries[8] and a chronology of presiding officers[9] have been compiled by Bertha Wilson and published in the *AHIL Quarterly*. Final division status was achieved by AHIL in 1944.

On 3 March 1931 Congress passed the first legislation bringing library service to the blind through books in Braille, and in 1934 the now famous talking books became available postage-free to any visually handicapped person.

During the early part of the twentieth century many large tuberculosis sanatoria were built; this group of long-term patients had a need for therapeutic library services. Many public libraries added hospital visits as a part of their extension services. The Cleveland Public Library developed a noteworthy program, which was publicized in the film *The Winged Bequest*.[10]

World War II brought a revitalization of library services to the armed forces and to the veterans' hospitals. At this time, however, other forms of activity therapy were coming to the fore. Departments for these specialized therapies were established in every large hospital, and courses were inaugurated to train workers in these ancillary professions. So for a time, with attention demanded elsewhere, interest in hospital libraries waned. The lack of trained personnel resulted in inadequate staffing; hospital service by public libraries was reorganized or curtailed, and in some instances discontinued.

However, with the broadening of therapies, the need for bibliotherapy increased, and spread into educational and psychosocial areas. The use of counselors in schools led to recognition of the psychological handicaps which impede learning, and in many cases children were guided to solutions for emotional or behavior problems through prescribed reading followed by discussion. Also, frustrations resulting from lack of social development have been brought to light through work with the disadvantaged in antipoverty and other community programs. The resources of storefront and branch libraries have been strengthened to bring helpful literature closer to those in need, and professional help on many levels has been provided. This approaches the type of service offered in hospitals and institutions where the librarian is fully involved in remediation and rehabilitation. With all types of state institutions providing service to the physically handicapped, to the mentally ill and mentally retarded, and to those in correctional institutions, the pattern of library service had to be broken out of its conventional shell, and brought to the level of the institutionalized patron.

A landmark publication in the field of bibliotherapy was Caroline Shrodes' doctoral dissertation in 1949.[11] Her theoretical and clinical study demonstrated the use of bibliotherapy as a treatment method in psychotherapy.

In 1959 a poetry therapy group was organized at the Mental Hygiene Clinic of Cumberland Hospital, Brooklyn, under Eli Greifer. Since that time similar groups have been established in many hospitals and clinics, and the movement has spread significantly.

In October 1962, as mentioned in the Preface, an issue of *Library Trends* devoted entirely to bibliotherapy was published, with Ruth M. Tews as editor.[12] As a follow-up of this issue, a workshop on bibliotherapy was held in conjunction with the American Library Association's annual conference at Saint Louis in 1964. This workshop was noteworthy because of its wide professional base. Participating were representatives from the related fields of psychiatry, clinical psychology, psychiatric nursing, and social work; practitioners of recreational, activity, and occupational therapy; librarians representing differing areas of service and, by invitation, observers from 32 related agencies. The workshop was sponsored by the American Library Association under a grant from the National Institute of Mental Health.

The proceedings of this workshop were published as an expanded issue of the *AHIL Quarterly*.[13]

In June 1966 the Library Services and Construction Act Title IV-A, for improved state institution library services, and Title IV-B, for improved services to the physically handicapped, were passed by Congress. State library administrative agencies were authorized to administer these funds, with the first year's appropriations being for planning only. Subsequent funding has resulted in upgrading facilities and services, and should eventually lead to an expansion of therapeutic library services both within state institutions and to the physically handicapped in the community. Also in 1966 a federal grant was awarded to the Public Library. of Cincinnati and Hamilton County for a two-year demonstration of library service to exceptional children. Miss Hilda Limper was named director. From this demonstration a film, *Reaching Out: The Library and the Exceptional Child,* was made.[14]

In February 1967 the Medical and General Reference Library of the Veterans Administration published a classified and annotated bibliography under the title *We Call It Bibliotherapy*.[15] This includes literature on bibliotherapy for adult hospitalized patients published from 1900 to 1966. Also in 1967 Vera S. Flandorf compiled a notable list entitled *Books to Help Children Adjust to a Hospital Situation*.[16]

In recent years bibliotherapy has been explored as an adjunct to sociology and education. Val Clear, chairman of the Department of Sociology and Social Work, Anderson College, Anderson, Indiana, has used fiction and biography in his classes to develop attitudes, not merely to present facts. His material was published by the New York State Library as a suggested library-sponsored program for communities involved in the war on poverty.[17] Presenting both a psychological and sociological point of view is *Mirror for Adjustment* by Austin Porterfield.[18] This is a revision of an earlier edition entitled *Mirror, Mirror: On Seeing Yourself in Books*. The educational point of view is found in *Facilitating Human Development through Reading: The Use of Bibliotherapy in Teaching and Counseling,* published in 1968 by Zaccaria and Moses.[19] In 1969 *Poetry Therapy,* edited by Jack J. Leedy, M.D., was published.[20] This book traces the development of the poetry therapy movement, proposes a national association of poetry therapists, and offers a curriculum for training such therapists.

This continuing and varied interest in bibliotherapy and the expansion of therapeutic library services points up the need for gathering quantitative data, and for evaluating the methods and materials currently in use. Thorough research may demonstrate whether or not it is possible to systematize the practice of bibliotherapy, and show where its use is indicated or contraindicated. Zaccaria and Moses point out that bibliotherapy does not replace other techniques, and that it cannot be used with all persons for all purposes.[21]

What Is Bibliotherapy?

Although bibliotherapy has been known and practiced since ancient times, the term itself is of more recent origin. It is generally credited to Samuel McChord Crothers in an article in *Atlantic Monthly* in 1916, in which he quotes a friend as saying, "Bibliotherapy is such a new science that it is no wonder that there are many erroneous opinions as to the actual effect which any particular book may have."[22]

The term was first defined in *Dorland's Illustrated Medical Dictionary* in 1941 as "The employment of books and the reading of them in the treatment of nervous disease."[23] In the issue of *Library Trends* devoted to bibliotherapy, Tews presented a composite statement based on the results of a questionnaire: "Bibliotherapy is a program of selected activity involving reading materials, planned, conducted, and controlled as treatment under the guidance of the physician for emotional and other problems."[24] Menninger and others compared its use to that of pharmacology: reading materials are withheld or prescribed as specifically as medications with the expectation of predictable results. Departing somewhat from the clinical aspects, Shrodes defines bibliotherapy as "a process of interaction between the personality of the reader and imaginative literature which may engage his emotions and free them for conscious and productive use."[25]

The Association of Hospital and Institution Libraries has adopted as official the dictionary definition, which reads: "the use of selected reading materials as therapeutic adjuvants in medicine and in psychiatry; *also,* guidance in the solution of personal problems through directed reading." The Association also accepts the dictionary definition of therapy: "treatment of the maladjusted . . . to further their restoration to society; a force working to relieve a social tension."[26] This allows for a broad interpretation of the term "bibliotherapy," and for its use in social and educational areas as well as in psychiatry and medicine.

A Rationale of Bibliotherapy

For many persons the written word has exceptional authority and authenticity. Evidence of the extent to which individuals look to reading material for help with personal problems and concerns is prevalent. Most literate people can mention at least one or two books which have affected them profoundly, which have expanded their potential for growth and development, and have provided not only instruction and knowledge but also understanding and inspiration.

To many people books have simply prestige value. To others they may be of value for information and instruction or may assist in the processes of socialization by providing something that can be shared and discussed with others. Books also may provide language and ideas by means of which the individual can clarify his problems.

The current mounting stress upon all aspects of mental health, in both the public and the private sector, has resulted in an interest in therapeutic reading on the part of librarians, educators, physicians, social workers, psychologists, and, indeed, all members of the community associated in any way with guiding any aspect of interpersonal relationships. Literature displays the dynamics of psychology in its concern with emotion and tensions. Stone and Stone, in their introduction to *The Abnormal Personality through Literature,* speak of the ability of Dostoevsky, the Russian novelist, to transform and enlarge the reader's world:

> [His] awesome talents were poured into "biographies," as he portrayed motives, feelings, passions, the good and evil, all of human nature that was accessible to his gift. Dostoevsky is only one of the literary greats who turned his talents toward "biography," and thus "fiction" has paradoxically become one of the richest and most profound sources of man's realistic view of man.[27]

Kiell, in *The Adolescent through Fiction,* tells us:

> The work of the novelist can help tremendously toward understanding the adolescent of today. For the first-rate writers get their sense of life from life, not from psychology books. . . . While literature and psychology are fellow disciplines, literature is not watered-down psychology nor is psychology methodized literature."[28]

In analyzing the therapeutic value of poetry, Schauffler states that psychic mechanisms are set in motion when the poet composes a poem which affects the reader in the same way he was affected: these are mechanisms of escape, of self-defense, and of compensation. He marvels that the poem which is created by the poet for therapeutic purposes will very often provide the same relief for the reader.[29] In this same vein, Leedy recommends that the therapist choose verse that will be useful to psychotherapy. Even inferior poetry may be helpful or right for a patient, and may be his bridge to reality, so that literary quality is not a criterion; the only consideration is whether or not the poem will help to heal the ill.[30]

There is difficulty in locating and categorizing the material which brings insight and change of attitude, however. It is this ability to analyze literature and its communicative effects that the librarian must develop and use in therapy. The criteria for standard book selection practices cannot always be followed, a fact which disturbs many librarians. The Association of Hospital and Institution Libraries has found it necessary to formulate a statement regarding the selection of materials which emphasizes this point: "Interest takes precedence over prestige or literary value."[31] It is not that the librarian has lowered his standards for judging literature, but that the circumstances governing use of the material necessitate the choice, and this is actually a more sophisticated form of book selection. The librarian, putting aside his own tastes, standards, and professional training, meets the reader on his educational and cultural level, because it is only in this context that communication is possible. This approach may account for the success of Fader's program described in *Hooked on Books*.[32] Not only is the selection of material affected; the relationship between the librarian and the reader is altered as well.

Monroe defines reader services as "those face-to-face as well as bibliographic services tailored to the individual reader or to him and his kind in a specific situation." She lists three basic techniques which are utilized in reader services:

1. Information technique places the needed data in the hands of the reader, with the work of selection, evaluation, and interpretation done by the librarian.
2. Instructional technique shows the reader how to use the library tools, and provides him with the skills he needs to secure the information or to select his books for reading.
3. Guidance technique assists the reader in his choice of library materials by interpreting a variety of suitable materials in terms of their relevance to the reader's interests and needs. It is in this area that the field of bibliotherapy has developed, and bibliotherapy is subject to the same general principles as is all of reading guidance.[33]

This concept of reading guidance goes only part of the way in meeting the needs of readers in hospitals and institutions. Bibliotherapy presupposes an extension of reader guidance, in which the librarian must demonstrate a particular concern for the psychological, sociological, and educational needs of the reader, and must be trained to recognize and deal with his problems. In his professional training the librarian develops a tendency to become book-oriented rather than client-oriented, and he may lack the ability to understand and deal with the individual who finds himself, for one reason or another, in an institution. Modern institutional care is no longer merely custodial; its goals and objectives include the triad of educational, sociological, and psychological gains. The librarian who is not involved in these objectives will find himself and his library on the periphery of the total institutional program.

It is the handicapped, the disadvantaged, the socially inadequate, who most often find themselves in institutions, and it is these individuals who lack the normal development of living skills, life functions, or whatever name one wishes to use. Dr. Nathan G. Mandel, Director of Research for the Minnesota Department of Corrections, has found that 80 percent of offenders lack living skills, while 80–85 percent have never had adequate work training or a work history that is based on self-support for a period of one year.[34] Where these people are concerned, it is not enough for the librarian to take a passive role. These persons may not be aware of their deficiencies, or they may be completely indifferent to or resentful of the idea of change. The librarian in this situation must attempt to stimulate interest and create a desire to learn and to change. This change of attitude occurs through emotional response to a person-to-person or person-to-book confrontation, but the individual can respond only within the range of his own capability. That is why the selection of suitable materials and their use, particularly on the low reading-high interest level, present very real problems for the institution librarian.

In the educational field reading has previously been defined as the ability to recognize words and to verbalize. According to Lohmann, the present definition includes verbalization, comprehension, interpretation, and evaluation. He indicates that there are several levels of concern that the librarian must take into account. The first is the functional reading level; second, the interest level; third, the satisfaction level, which is indicated by the frequency with which the reader uses the library; and fourth, the capacity level, the amount of material it takes to satisfy the reader's intellectual curiosity.[35] In addition, the librarian needs to know something of the visual ability, the personality, and the vocational and avocational level of the reader.

The library setting is known to exert a subtle influence. Long before the term "environmental therapy" came into common use, the library was known to have a salutary effect on patients and inmates. In some measure this may be attributed to the fact that the library is nonclinical in appearance, and that it is one of the few areas in an institution which has a familiar counterpart in the outside world. Using the library indicates that the individual is capable of some measure of mental functioning, that he is sufficiently intact to be able to pursue his interests independently and without supervision, or that he may join with others in groups to explore his problems by interpreting them through reading and discussing literature. The term "the unwounded area" has been used to express the fact that only certain areas of a person's mental makeup may be affected and need treatment; in other respects he may function normally. More attention needs to be given to strengthening these unwounded areas.

Reading for enjoyment and relaxation is so taken for granted that its power to develop and strengthen wholesome attitudes is often overlooked. In the regimented atmosphere of an institution the ability to obtain a direction for oneself by choosing one's own reading and losing oneself in a book can be, but should not be, a luxury.

In any evaluation of personality there are conclusions to be drawn from a comparison of the reader and nonreader. The nonreader is deprived of an important avenue of communication, so that his attitudes and insights are stifled rather than stimulated. An alert librarian may be able to appeal to his intellectual curiosity in a nondirective way by presenting him with a choice of materials on various subjects, written on a level which he can understand and appreciate. When a response occurs, it is a gratifying experience, and the individual is given the incentive to expand his interests further.

Notes

1. W. B. McDaniel II, "Bibliotherapy: Some Historical and Contemporary Aspects," *ALA Bulletin* 50:584–89 (Oct. 1956).

2. W. K. Beatty, "A Historical Review of Bibliotherapy," *Library Trends* 11:106–17 (Oct. 1962).

3. R. M. Tews, "Bibliotherapy," in Allen Kent and Harold Lancour, eds., *Encyclopedia of Library and Information Science* (New York: Marcel Dekker, 1969), 2: 448–57.

4. P. J. Weimerskirch, "Benjamin Rush and John Minson Galt, II—Pioneers of Bibliotherapy in America," *Bulletin of the Medical Library Association* 53:510–26 (1965).

5. Elizabeth Pomeroy, "Bibliotherapy—A Study in Results of Hospital Library Service," *Medical Bulletin of the Veterans Administration* 13:360–64 (April 1937).

6. Perrie Jones, "Survey of Hospital Libraries Abroad and at Home," *Transactions of the American Hospital Association* 36:360–68 (1934).

7. E. K. Jones, *The Hospital Library* (Chicago: American Library Assn., 1923).

8. B. I. Wilson, "History of AHIL," *AHIL Quarterly 8:48–54* (Winter 1968).

9. ———. "Presiding Officers of AHIL and Its Predecessors," *AHIL Quarterly* 8:109–12 (Summer 1968).

10. *The Winged Bequest.* A 16mm film produced by Edward Feil Productions. 1955. Sound, color, 22 min. Sponsored by the Cleveland Public Library and Cleveland Foundation.

11. Caroline Shrodes, "Bibliotherapy: A Theoretical and Clinical-Experimental Study" (Ph.D. dissertation, Univ. of California at Berkeley, 1949).

12. R. M. Tews, ed., "Bibliotherapy," *Library Trends* v.11, no.2 (Oct. 1962).

13. W. K. Beatty, ed., "Proceedings of the ALA Bibliotherapy Workshop, St. Louis, June 25–27, 1964," *AHIL Quarterly*, v.4 (Summer 1964).

14. *Reaching Out: The Library and the Exceptional Child.* A 16mm film produced by Connecticut Films, Inc., Westport, Conn., 1969. Sound, color, 25 min.

15. U.S. Veterans Administration, Medical and General Reference Library, *We Call It Bibliotherapy: An Annotated Bibliography on Bibliotherapy and the Adult Hospitalized Patient, 1900–1966* (Washington, D.C.: Veterans Administration, 1967).

16. V. S. Flandorf, *Books to Help Children Adjust to a Hospital Situation* (Chicago: American Library Assn., 1967).

17. New York State Library, Library Extension Division, *The Disadvantaged: A Program for Understanding* (Rev. ed.; Albany, N.Y.: (The Library, 1966).

18. A. E. Porterfield, *Mirror for Adjustment: Therapy in Home, School, and Society through Seeing Yourself and Others in Books* (Fort Worth, Tex.: Leo Potishman Foundation, Texas Christian Univ., 1967).

19. J. S. Zaccaria and H. A. Moses, *Facilitating Human Development through Reading: The Use of Bibliotherapy in Teaching and Counseling* (Champaign, Ill.: Stipes, 1968).

20. J. J. Leedy, ed., *Poetry Therapy: The Use of Poetry in the Treatment of Emotional Disorders* (Philadelphia: Lippincott, 1969).

21. Zaccaria and Moses, *Facilitating Human Development through Reading*, p.83.

22. S. M. Crothers, "A Literary Clinic," *Atlantic Monthly* 118:291–301 (Aug. 1916).

23. *Dorland's Illustrated Medical Dictionary* (19th ed.; Philadelphia: Saunders, 1941).

24. R. M. Tews, "Introduction," *Library Trends* 11:97–105 (Oct. 1962).

25. Caroline Shrodes, "Bibliotherapy: An Application of Psychoanalytic Theory," *American Imago* 17:311–19 (Fall 1960).

26. *Webster's Third New International Dictionary* (Springfield, Mass.: Merriam, 1961).

27. A. A. Stone and S. S. Stone, eds., *The Abnormal Personality through Literature* (Englewood Cliffs, N.J.: Prentice-Hall, 1966), p.vii.

28. Norman Kiell, *The Adolescent through Fiction: A Psychological Approach* (New York: International Universities Pr., 1959), p.14.

29. R. H. Schauffler, *The Poetry Cure* (New York: Dodd, 1927), p.xxiii.

30. J. J. Leedy, ed., *Poetry Therapy*, p.72.

31. Association of Hospital and Institution Libraries, Special Committee on Book Selection Criteria, *Materials Selection for Hospital and Institution Libraries* (Chicago: American Library Assn., 1967).

32. D. N. Fader and E. B. McNeil, *Hooked on Books: Program and Proof* (New York: Berkley, 1968).

33. M. E. Monroe, "Reader Services and Bibliotherapy" (paper presented at the Institute on Serving Readers through Hospital and Institution Libraries, University of Wisconsin-Madison, 7–20 July 1968).

34. N. G. Mandel, Unpublished paper presented at the Upper Midwest Hospital Association Conference, Minneapolis, 10 May 1968.

35. V. L. Lohmann, "Special Reading Needs of Library Users," *Minnesota Libraries* 22:165–69 (Summer 1968).

Dynamics

Operative Principles

Before bibliotherapy as a technique can be systematized, it is advisable to define attainable psychological goals, to devise the processes by which these goals can be reached, and to determine tests which will measure the results achieved. This type of research has been applied to the development of reading skills, and both methods and materials are under constant scrutiny in education. There are only isolated reports of the same careful planning for bibliotherapy.

Reading as therapy appears best suited for disturbances having an extrapsychic origin. In discussing the background of group psychotherapy, Slavson traces its development from 1905, when a class method of "thought control" clinics was started with a group of patients suffering from pulmonary tuberculosis.[1] This procedure was successful in dealing with the problems inherent in the illness, and with the mental attitudes of these and other long-term patients. However, when the method was tried with the mentally ill, it was found that education and instruction were not effective, because the intrapsychic structure of the patient has to be the focus of the therapeutic effort. Intrapsychic tensions must be removed before re-education of the emotions is possible. While education, suggestion, guidance, and advice may be useful in dealing with some kinds of adjustment problems, they should not be confused with real psychotherapy, which is aimed at effecting changes in the personality structure.

It is important to understand that the intellect has little to do with the therapeutic process. Personality changes occur through emotional experience in transference, and not through teaching and learning. Of all the factors which are involved in the dynamics of psychotherapy, those which apply to bibliotherapy are universalization, identification, catharsis, and insight. Feelings of inadequacy, guilt, and shame are diluted through universalization, and social attitudes and values are formed through identification.[2] Through the two together, self-protectiveness is weakened and self-esteem becomes stronger. Catharsis is the outward expression or purging of repressed material. In the adult this is usually done by talking; children more often resort to action. Catharsis may give the patient temporary relief, but emotional maturity is achieved through insight. In a group patients may induce insight in one another through the presentation of common problems and the interpretation of one another's motives. These are not group insights, but changes of attitude in each individual through the group process. The individual, not the group, is always the focus of the therapeutic effort. This is the psychotherapeutic basis upon which bibliotherapy rests. Shrodes writes:

> Reading, like all other human behavior, is a function of the total personality. When we read fiction, poetry, or drama, we perceive selectively in accordance with our needs, goals, defenses, and values. Parallel in substance and function to the primary phases of psychotherapy, the vicarious experience induced by reading includes identification, projection and introjection, transference of emotion from early experience to current symbols of it, catharsis, and insight. However, the reader will abstract from the work of art only what he is able to perceive and organize. . . . Imaginative literature provides an external frame of reference which permits the reader to view his experience freshly from the perspective of the detached observer. Being at once fantasy and reality, it permits the reader to be both participant and spectator.[3]

Freud describes the power of the imaginative writer to redirect the emotions of the reader. He speaks of this power as a peculiarly directive influence by which the writer is able to guide the current of our emotions, to dam it up in one direction and make it flow in another.[4] Shrodes comments that a situation in a story may be so compelling that it becomes interchanged in the reader's mind with an episode in his own life, and that the patient who may not be able to talk directly about his own feelings and experiences may reveal them indirectly when talking about fictional characters.

The development of a standardized technique and the training of bibliotherapists has been undertaken at the Agnews State Hospital in California. This library project began by using a physician as therapist, with the librarian acting as a resource person analyzing and selecting material to be used in group reading sessions. Other staff members came to observe, and subsequently became group leaders. A report of the project indicates that bibliotherapy has had wide acceptance by both staff and patients, and that it is expected to become a continuing part of the library program.[5]

The loose definition of bibliotherapy is favored by variations of the standard pattern. For example, several authors suggest that reading groups or individual reading programs be used to create a state of readiness for psychotherapeutic counseling. Brammer and Shostrom call this type of informational reading "bibliotherapy." They cite several benefits to both the patient and therapist. First, reading saves time because it satisfies the individual's need for specific information and frees the counselor for more essential instruction. Second, it provides the patient with the terminology of mental hygiene and of emotions in general, so that he can express his feelings and ideas in more explicit language. Third, it stimulates thinking and amplifies the insight which the patient is receiving from his counselor. Fourth, it enables the counselor to give support as his guidance continues outside of counseling sessions through reading. However, the authors also warn against some of the apparent limitations of bibliotherapy. For instance, readiness for counseling could be reduced because people tend to rationalize their problems when they read about them. Another hazard is that the reader often thinks that the reading is helping him solve his problem, and he may substitute the vicarious insight obtained from reading for the genuine growth to be gained from the counseling relationship. Finally, patients with weak defenses acquire more symptoms and reinforce their anxieties by reading about mental health problems.[6]

On this same subject Goldstein and associates write:

> With an eye toward increasing the efficiency of therapy we are inclined to suggest the use of written and tape-recorded material rather than having the therapist spend his time covering the same ground. Bibliotherapy has usually had the form of stimulating reading of the "self help" variety. We would like to see material made available for the specific purpose of preparing the prospective patient for psychotherapy by presenting a theory relevant to his disorder, a rationale for treatment, and a description of the treatment to follow.[7]

Bibliotherapy as preparation for psychotherapy may be conducted on an individual or group basis, and is a natural function of the library. To an apprehensive person approaching therapy, the library is a neutral, non-threatening area in which books and other familiar reading matter are used. The reader may develop a reliance on the library's resources to reinforce counseling, but care must be taken to provide only those materials that will adequately support his treatment.

The verbalization function has been stressed by Penny. She has introduced a three-stage form of bibliotherapy, the objective of which is to develop verbalization in uncommunicative patients. She employs factual material, without dialogue, in an effort to stimulate reading of a few words or sentences. The patient, through this activity, learns that he can speak without any ill effect, and overcomes his symptom of blocked speech. The second stage makes use of the same type of material, with the patient responding to questions with factual statements that do not require a personal opinion or emotional involvement. In the third stage material from a book or newspaper or a radio or television program is discussed, inviting personal opinion. The end result to be obtained through this progressive activity should be clearly defined by the therapist.[8] For the withdrawn patient these sessions are excellent preparation for later group participation, since they develop the ability to respond.

Reading as therapy for social problems focuses on the improvement of living skills, because the frustration and lack of self-esteem that accompany social and cultural deprivation lead to emotional and behavior problems. All aspects of daily living, but particularly those of home and family affairs, occupational adequacy, management of money and material, social amenities, and matters of health are likely subjects for discussion. More and more the institutional library is planning its functions toward development of these skills, and this is part of the total institution effort with interdisciplinary involvement. The sense of pride and accomplishment that accompanies the acquisition of these skills bears witness to the fact that therapeutic effects do occur when the individual is able to function more appropriately. He does not merely acquire information, but also is able to cope with circumstances as they arise; and consequently is happier.

The goals of education go far beyond the acquisition of basic skills and training for a vocation. Havighurst's theoretical formulation of developmental tasks is based upon the gradual progression that is normally expected to occur.[9] With those whom we presently call disadvantaged, with the retarded, and in cases of physical and mental disablement, this formative process does not take place at the appropriate time. Hopefully, remedial efforts will be undertaken to fill in the gaps. If the need is recognized quickly, the therapist's role is a preventive one; if the lack of normal development has persisted for some time, rehabilitative and therapeutic measures become necessary. Bibliotherapy, which includes both intellectual and emotional components, can help the reader make up for his loss, and promote personality growth.

Zaccaria and Moses stress the active and supportive roles of bibliotherapy in the developmental approach:

1. Although human growth and development are relatively continuous, the course of human development can be conveniently abstracted and described in terms of rather discrete developmental periods, or developmental stages.
2. Research in the behavioral sciences (psychology, social psychology,

sociology, anthropology) has resulted in the accumulation of enough knowledge about the course of human development so that practitioners can help individuals anticipate problems and crises, and therefore eliminate them before they occur in many cases.

3. Although many of the problems of youth can be prevented via a developmental approach to teaching and guidance, a focus upon remediation is required to complement the developmental (preventive) focus.[10]

Teaching the individual to learn involves a number of techniques which may create emotional stress: problem solving, motor and perceptual learning, symbolic learning, and learning by imitation. Learning by problem solving implies that obstacles must be dealt with, and that success comes only after trial and error. If the problem is beyond the individual's ability to solve, or if he has been overprotected or has lacked stimulus so that he does not rise to the challenge, frustrations occur which are beyond normal tolerance. Abstract learning, reasoning, develops slowly, and a great deal of guidance and understanding are necessary to help a child adapt his thought processes to reality. By using selected reading that goes to the heart of the problem, the pressures that arise from lack of understanding and underachievement may be relieved, and attention can be focused on actual learning.

Much of the current emphasis on the disadvantaged and the adult illiterate, many of whom are found in institutions, has dealt with improving the means by which the undereducated may be taught. In the 66th Yearbook of the National Society for the Study of Education, Witty describes some of the methods used with both children and adults, including the successful program used during World War II to instruct illiterate and non-English-speaking servicemen.[11] Witty has also described how reading can help the young to achieve a sense of identity by working through the basic developmental tasks of adolescence. Through their reading they learn the insights and behavior appropriate to their age before problems become pathological.[12]

In summary, psychotherapy often includes reading material that stimulates both the emotions and the intellect. Reading may be an adjunct to counseling, or it may prepare the patient for counseling. Based on a structure of developmental tasks, it may be a part of the social and educational process. Education and therapy are mutually reactive, and as Kubie writes:

> The state of being educated can be reached only if the learning experience is interwoven with continuous corrective influences from processes derived from formal psychotherapy but not identical with

it. An approach to this goal will also have to include a reassessment of what constitutes *educability* in a human being, emphasizing his emotional maturation as well as his intellectual capabilities to learn. We will have to recognize that emotional health and maturity are at least as essential for education as is the intelligence quotient, and that the idiot-savant and the absent-minded scholar provide evidence that the achievement of erudition does not bring affective maturity, which must be achieved in other ways.[13]

Therapeutic Communication

The interchange of thoughts and opinions known as communication goes far beyond speech or writing because such nonverbal means as touch, gesture, and facial expression account for a large share of conveyed meaning. Behavioral scientists tell us that communication is a precondition to all other activities. People initiate information, implement information, and are affected by information. Common to all communication is the sender-message-medium-receiver relationship. When every step of this process is without fault, the result, or feedback, is good. If one or more of these factors is weak, incorrect, or inappropriate, communication is distorted.

The success of psychotherapy rests on whether or not true communication occurs between therapist and client. In bibliotherapy, a third dimension is added. We have the author's ability to communicate with the reader, the reader's ability to comprehend and react to what he is reading, plus the therapist's skill in recognizing the change of attitude that is taking place and directing the current of thought toward the reader's awareness.

The dynamics of all communication, verbal or nonverbal, are based on the expectation of response to a stimulus. The words and the demeanor of the therapist are important in the relationship. Together they comprise the stimulus which is conveyed by the medium of language.

Slavson states that therapeutic communication in analytic psychotherapy must be verbal, and that one of the basic requirements is that the patient feel free to talk on any and all subjects and reveal his thoughts without reservation. He notes that everyone is vulnerable because of past failures or rejection, incidents which the person would rather not discuss, and he ascribes the term "threat areas" to those subjects which the person evades in ordinary conversation.[14]

Dealing with threat areas is the ultimate aim of therapeutic communication, and the barriers are often broken by the identification or catharsis which occurs through reading. It is necessary for the therapist to recognize this breakthrough, and direct the free expression of thought to the individual's problem. The therapist must be alert to the reader's tendency to evade and resist self-confrontation by talking in abstract rather than specific terms, and adhere to direct and detailed discussion of the subject which has been opened up. Generalities or philosophical principles should be used sparingly, and usually only to terminate a discussion which has been explicit, and which has attacked the individual's defenses.

The art of the writer consists of his ability to make symbolic use of minute details to convey his meaning. In bibliotherapy the art of the therapist consists of his ability to guide the person into an examination of the bits and pieces that have gone into the creation of his problem, and help him to express freely the insights which he has received. The reader responds emotionally to bibliotherapy only when he recognizes himself in the literature. This shock of recognition is the therapist's cue to bring the discussion to a personal level. The bibliotherapist must understand the principles which guide creative writing, the principles of communication, and those of psychotherapy to make the most effective use of his technique.

Notes

1. S. R. Slavson, *Analytic Group Psychotherapy with Children, Adolescents, and Adults* (New York: Columbia Univ. Pr., 1950), p.2.

2. Ibid., p.96–97.

3. Caroline Shrodes, "The Dynamics of Reading: Implications for Bibliotherapy," *Etc.: A Review of General Semantics* 18:21–33 (April 1961).

4. Sigmund Freud, *Collected Papers*, v.4 (London: International Psychoanalytical Pr., 1924), p. 405–6.

5. E. Steffens, "Agnews State Hospital Patients Library Bibliotherapy Project (1968–1969) (Unpublished report, project #3692, Title IV-A).

6. L. M. Brammer and E. L. Shostrom, *Therapeutic Psychology* (2d ed.; Englewood Cliffs, N.J.: Prentice-Hall, 1968), p.316-20.

7. A. P. Goldstein, K. Heller, and L. B. Sechrist, *Psychotherapy and the Psychology of Behavior Change* (New York: Wiley, 1966), p.250.

8. Ruthanna Penny, *Practical Care of the Mentally Retarded and Mentally Ill* (Springfield, Ill.: Thomas, 1966), p.171–76.

9. R. J. Havighurst, *Developmental Tasks and Education* (New York: Longmans, 1950).

10. J. S. Zaccaria and H. A. Moses, *Facilitating Human Development through Reading: The Use of Bibliotherapy in Teaching and Counseling* (Champaign, Ill.: Stipes, 1968), p.29.

11. P. A. Witty, "The Educability of Undereducated Americans," in Paul A. Witty, ed., *The Educationally Retarded and Disadvantaged*, 66th Yearbook of the National Society for the Study of Education (Chicago: Univ. of Chicago Pr., 1967), p.65–82.

12. ———. "Meeting Developmental Needs through Reading," *Education* 84:451–58 (1964).

13. L. S. Kubie, "The Psychotherapeutic Ingredient in the Learning Process," in R. Porter, ed., *The Role of Learning in Psychotherapy* (Boston: Little, 1968) p.232.

14. S. R. Slavson, *A Textbook in Analytical Group Psychotherapy* (New York: International Universities Pr., 1964) p.265–69.

Therapy

Individual Reader Guidance

In the hospital or institution the librarian's first contact with the patron is made soon after admission. The patient or inmate is met at a time when he is cut off from normal life; he may have suffered a debilitating illness or physical impairment, mental breakdown, or commitment by a court. Often he is full of fear and hostility, inwardly crying for help and understanding. There is never only one problem; it is common to find a combination of physical, mental, legal, social, financial, or familial problems, all needing the combined attention of the staff.

The patient's attitude toward the library and its services will be set to a considerable degree by his introduction to the collection and the library staff. Whether this takes place in the library or during a visit to the wards with a book cart, plenty of time should be devoted to orientation, to determine the needs and interests of the patient.

The ability to conduct an interview in a disarming and intelligent manner will help to establish good rapport. In assisting the individual reader the relationship of reference service, reader guidance, and bibliotherapy becomes apparent. In some instances the reader need only be directed to reference sources or a collection of material suggested by the librarian, or he may be instructed in the use of library tools to secure the information he needs. In this matter of reader guidance Monroe has stated, "Guidance technique assists the reader in his choice of library materials in terms of their relevance to the reader's interests and needs."[1] Both reference service and reader guidance take place on a rather impersonal level; the objectives are informational, the reader is capable of making his own judgments, and there is seldom a third person such as a counselor, doctor, or teacher involved.

With reader guidance at a deeper level than that indicated by Monroe, the need for information is supplemented by an additional need to solve the underlying physical, mental, or social problems that are creating stress. Thus, reader guidance takes on the overtones of therapy by reinforcing the institution's treatment program with independent reading, and this may be referred to as therapeutic library service. Actually, it falls within the dictionary definition of bibliotherapy, "the use of selected reading materials as therapeutic adjuvants in medicine and in psychiatry; *also,* guidance in the solution of personal problems through directed reading."

As an example, an amputee learns from the clinical staff about the physical details of his surgery, and other staff members take up the task of his rehabilitation. The question arises: Will he accept the reality of his condition, the change in his person and personality? Will he make the adjustments necessary to compensate for his loss? There is a wealth of published material which will help him face this dilemma. An interview with the librarian may determine what he should be reading to acquire additional information. Through the rehabilitation team and through independent reading, the amputee will be able to understand the physical change that has taken place, and to overcome the psychological barriers which stand in the way of his rehabilitation. By getting to know other amputees, in person and through reading, he learns that this is an experience shared by many others (universalization), and he will learn that he, too, can make adjustments as others have done (identification). He will share others' frustrations, trials, and errors (catharsis), and eventually he will acquire the insight which leads to reality, and will make a successful transition to the changed conditions that exist.

The success or failure of the initial interview may determine the extent to which the reader is helped. It is important that the interview be conducted with tact and skill, so that a maximum amount of information may be gathered with a minimum amount of effort. An interview is a shared experience between the interviewer and the respondent. Each is trying to influence the other. If the interview is properly conducted, it results in an easy flow of information; if improperly handled, the flow of communication is restricted or distorted.

Rogers identifies the qualities which are necessary for successful counseling, and these apply to the interviewer as well: warmth and responsiveness which make rapport possible; permissiveness in regard to expression of feeling; freedom from any type of pressure or coercion.[2] Kahn and Cannell explain:

> We may conclude that a basic condition for optimum communication is that the respondent perceive the interviewer as one who is likely to understand and accept him and what he has to say. The interviewer must be perceived as "within range"—that is, he must be seen as a person to whom the respondent's statements and experience will

not be foreign or offensive. This does not mean that the respondent needs to see the interviewer as similar to himself, but he must view the interviewer as capable of understanding his point of view, and of doing so without rejecting him. This perception will depend far more on the interviewer's attitudes and the relation he establishes than on such external factors as dress or appearance, although these may be cues for the respondent.[3]

As the librarian seeks to learn the nature and extent of the reader's needs, the functional reading level, visual ability, and interest level must be determined. Satisfaction and capacity levels may be determined later. Additional background information may be obtained from consulting with staff members, or by attending staff conferences. Access to records is limited, and although in some instances it may seem desirable, it is not essential for the librarian to consult confidential records.

Unwillingness to listen carefully is the most frequent barrier to a good interview; inattention, rushing the respondent, or misunderstanding the response will close off further communication. On the other hand, the respondent may not understand the interviewer, or he may be hesitant or suspicious and therefore guarded in his replies.

There are four main requirements of a good listener: concentration, which is based on the removal of distractions; active participation, which involves keeping the mind in a state of relaxed alertness, open and flexible to change; comprehension, understanding and grasping the true meaning of what is being heard; and objectivity, the ability to hear the other person out without imposing preconceived notions or opinions. Interviewing skill may be developed through role playing, or by taping interviews on a tape recorder or on videotape for playback and critical study.

If the reader reveals information that is of diagnostic value or solicits aid that the librarian is not competent to give, an appropriate staff member should be informed so that this may be followed up. Records should be kept of interviews, and of the reading which follows. Significant details should be reported at staff meetings so that they may become a part of the individual's record, and should be taken into account in an evaluation of his progress.

Group Bibliotherapy

Group therapy has become a widely used technique in hospitals and institutions, in private practice, rehabilitation, counseling, education, industry, and other situations. The term was coined by J. L. Moreno,[4] who also provided leadership to the group psychotherapy movement since its inception early in the twentieth century. Since that time the effectiveness of well-run therapy groups has been documented by many writers.

In the beginning the group method was used primarily as a substitute for individual therapy when large case loads did not allow time for individual sessions. As knowledge of the group process increased, it was realized that group dynamics differ from those of individual analysis or counseling. A unique atmosphere, democratic rather than authoritarian, is created by interaction between the members of the group and the group leader. Participation provides the opportunity for breaking down emotional isolation as the members try to help one another. There is also a learning process in which members gain insight from other members as well as from the leader. The discussion leads to identification with one another's feelings, and the individuals find strength through shared experiences. Alcoholics Anonymous and other similar groups encourage a type of open confession or public disclosure which has a cathartic effect. Through mutual sharing and support a sense of equality develops. Moreover, in contending with the attitudes of his peers, the person tests himself in situations which have real social meaning, and this reality testing has a significant effect on the value system of each participant.

In *Group Therapy: A Guide,* Luchins reviews the development of group therapy but is unable to define it because "no generally accepted definition exists."[5] He sees the diversity of concepts and methods not as signs of confusion or ignorance but rather as an indication of the interest and activity of many people in this field. Their willingness to try different methods and formulate new concepts has resulted in a healthy growth of the discipline.

Throughout his book Luchins delineates the role of the group therapist under a variety of circumstances. The therapist is the key figure in group therapy, and what he is determines the type of group he will lead and the methods he will use. In his survey of the literature extending over two decades Luchins discovered that "psychiatrists, clinical psychologists, social workers, ministers, nurses, aides, occupational therapists, and the like all have been engaged in group therapy either alone or with other professionals."[6] He concludes that nearly everyone could, with special training and supervision, engage in therapy, but indicates the necessity for the therapist to define his professional domain and demonstrate his competence for a special kind of therapy.

Group bibliotherapy is also difficult to define because the ways in which patients benefit from books and other media and from group experiences are as varied as people themselves. The methods of the bibliotherapist may be as individual as those of other group therapists. However, if workers accept this diversity as an opportunity for development, experimentation, and research, they will be instrumental in making bibliotherapy more generally available.

The librarian-therapist's professional domain includes a wide acquaintance with literature and other media, an interest in and understanding of group processes, and skill as a reader's adviser. In addition, according to Kinney, the bibliotherapist needs the personal qualifications, the emotional stability, the physical well-being, the character and personality necessary for him to work successfully with people.[7]

Since formal courses in bibliotherapy are not yet available, competence in this specific kind of therapy must be gained by all possible means, including courses in psychology, counseling, and group dynamics. Hannigan describes the training opportunities in institutions themselves;[8] Kinney indicates courses and on-the-job field experience for graduate-level training in bibliotherapy;[7] and both emphasize the value of the interdisciplinary approach for training purposes and for integrating bibliotherapy into the total therapy program.

A plan which has significance for the future training of bibliotherapists is the curriculum proposed by Edgar and Hazley for training poetry therapists, which would lead to certification in poetry therapy. The authors suggest undergraduate courses in psychology and English, graduate studies in the areas of psychology and literature, training in group therapy, and internship at a hospital.[9]

In spite of the latitude allowed in almost all aspects of group bibliotherapy, the librarian, whether he is a group bibliotherapist, a coleader of the group, or a resource person, has a definite role as a member of the interdisciplinary team in planning, reporting, and evaluating the progress of the group. He has the major responsibility for selecting materials for use in the group, for providing related materials for the members to read outside the group sessions, for discussing books, interests, and ideas with the readers, and for keeping records of the meetings.

The first step in starting a therapy group is defining its objectives. In *Strategy of Therapy* Tate covers the entire range of therapy from its theory to its practice. He makes the point that theory and strategy define the objectives while method and technique help in reaching these objectives, and observes that there are usually many ways to reach a goal. What is important is to define the objective so clearly that various ways of reaching it can be tried and compared. It follows that it is essential for the members of the therapy team to understand the various types of therapy represented in the institution. In the case of group bibliotherapy the unique contribution which the librarian and the library can make will be the determining factors.[10]

Library group activities can be coordinated with group therapy or serve directly as group therapy. They may range from reading-discussion or play-reading groups whose aims are simply enjoyment and socialization to group bibliotherapy aimed at helping members through identification, catharsis, and insight, or having other therapeutic goals. The materials of bibliotherapy are drawn from the whole field of human knowledge: imaginative literature; educational and informational materials, including popular psychology books and articles, biographies, history, science, and folklore; and a variety of others, including, as well as the printed word, film, recordings, and pictures. The methods include reading aloud individually or in unison; listening to a storyteller, a reader, or recordings; and always discussion.

Luchins suggests various types of literature to be used in group therapy and raises several questions regarding goals: for example, shall we be concerned with the expressive function of activities and the emotional release they provide, or shall we be concerned with decision making and reality testing? Since both principles are of value, it is important for the therapist to decide on the specific purpose for which each is to be applied. Luchins sees bibliotherapy as stimulating other activities such as role playing, psychodrama, or creative writing.[11]

Records and reports have already been mentioned. Generally two kinds of records are kept. The first kind is the actual recording or transcript of a session, including videotape, which may be used with the participants or by the staff. These are sometimes enriched by the therapist's comments. The second is records of individual participation, which, if they are of value for the patient's case history, are put into his treatment record. Changes will be indicated by adequate records as patients become ready for other types of therapy. There should be progression so that the same groups do not go on ad infinitum.

Experience has shown that group therapy can be conducted in almost any place where the members may interact with one another without interference, even though the spaciousness of the room, its atmosphere, comfortable furniture, and attractive furnishings do help to create a setting which in itself is therapeutic. The library is often an ideal place for meeting, because even in a treatment-oriented institution, it is readily identified with the library in the outside world, a place where well people go. Books and libraries, as the embodiment of our heritage and as a means of education and self-improvement, have important symbolic and practical significance for many people. This intangible yet real influence contributes to the therapeutic overtones of library group meetings.

In making the immense potential of group bibliotherapy easily available as one of the accepted methods of treatment, the bibliotherapist will select those methods and materials which will stimulate free expression, and create attitudes of sharing and helping, trust and confidence. The therapist must be wholly concerned with the progress each participant is making through group interaction, and must eventually judge when it is time to terminate this phase of therapy. Group members will then be directed into some other appropriate activity, but each member should be encouraged to continue an individual reading program, using the skills he has learned in group bibliotherapy to extract the meaning and insight each author has written into his literary work.

Notes

1. M. E. Monroe, "Reader Services and Bibliotherapy" (paper presented at the Institute on Serving Readers through Hospital and Institution Libraries, University of Wisconsin-Madison, 7-20 July 1968).

2. C. R. Rogers, *Counseling and Psychotherapy* (Boston: Houghton, 1942), p.87–89.

3. R. L. Kahn and C. F. Cannell, *The Dynamics of Interviewing* (New York: Wiley, 1957), p.47–48.

4. G. M. Gazda, ed., *Basic Approaches to Group Psychotherapy and Group Counseling* (Springfield, Ill.: C. C. Thomas, 1968), p.7.

5. A. S. Luchins, *Group Therapy: A Guide* (New York, Random, 1964), p.11–13.

6. Ibid., p.131.

7. M. M. Kinney, "The Bibliotherapy Program: Requirements for Training," *Library Trends* 11:127–35 (Oct. 1962).

8. M. C. Hannigan, "The Librarian in Bibliotherapy: Pharmacist or Bibliotherapist?", *Library Trends* 11:184–98 (Oct. 1962).

9. K. F. Edgar and R. Hazley, "A Curriculum Proposal for Training Poetry Therapists," in J. J. Leedy, ed., *Poetry Therapy,* (Philadelphia: Lippincott, 1969), p.60–68.

10. G. T. Tate, *Strategy of Therapy: Toward the Engineering of Social Growth* (New York, Springer Pub., 1967), p.119–26.

11. Luchins, *Group Therapy,* p.71–74.

There is a wide dissimilarity among the hospitals and institutions which provide library service for their residents. The library user may be an acute or chronically ill person in a private or governmental hospital, or he may be a resident in a nursing home. He may be a patient in a tax-supported state institution for the mentally ill or mentally retarded, or a student in a special school maintained for the education of the deaf and blind. Those in trouble with the law are found in correctional schools and prisons. There are institutions and halfway houses for those under treatment for alcohol and drug addiction.

First of all, every approach must be utilized to help the individual overcome the primary cause of his institutionalization. Second, one must consider the conditions in his life which contributed to his present state, and how these can be corrected. Also, what new problems are being created while the patient is in the institution which must be solved before he returns to the community? These are questions which must be faced when an institution assumes the care of these persons, and all departments, including the library, must be concerned with improving the level of patient or inmate care.

Before planning therapeutic library services, it is necessary for the librarian to understand the nature of these varied conditions, and the inherent social and psychological problems involved. There are other disabilities which merit discussion, but the following are the main groups served by hospital and institution libraries.

The Physically III

The most familiar health care facility in any community is the public or private hospital which services the needs of the physically ill. There may be a section for psychiatric, tuberculous, or other long-term patients, but in the main these institutions serve patients whose stay is relatively brief, and bibliotherapy in the usual sense is not undertaken, although hospital library service may be classed as a special type of activity therapy.

With the advent of television in hospital rooms and with the shortened stay of most patients, there has been a decline in support for library service to hospitals. It is argued that this is diversionary service only, and on the face of it this may be so, but there are deeper considerations. Many patients enter the hospital with fears and apprehensions which complicate the work of the clinical staff. To quote Dr. Hans Mauksch, "Shucked of his clothes, his identity, and, he feels, his rights, the patient feels lost in the hospital."[1]

There are several reasons why library service should be available to hospitalized persons: to counteract the dehumanizing effects of a hospital stay, to prevent regression, and to provide a link to the outside world; to demonstrate the hospital's concern for the total person, his recreational, social, and psychological needs; to inform the patient, when necessary, about the nature of his disease or disability; and to disseminate health care materials.

The dehumanizing effect arises in some measure from the necessary invasion of personal privacy. Hospital routine is not the commonplace, everyday occurrence to the patient that it is to the staff, and the staff's supposed lack of consideration is resented by the patient. In writing about the patient on prolonged bed rest Kottke says:

> Progressive intellectual and emotional deterioration occurs during prolonged bed rest. Multiple factors contribute to this psychological deterioration. The relative isolation of the patient from intellectual stimulation, the sensory deprivation, the forced dependency that promotes the development of a progressively increasing dependency, and the loss of a personal sense of worth are psychological values difficult to counteract while the patient is restricted to bed. . . . The patient experiences not only a deterioration in intellectual performance but a progressive decrease in emotional stability. The mutual problems are mutually reinforcing.[2]

Dr. Kottke recommends reading among other activities which help to maintain the patient's level of performance.

Some disabling conditions may involve the librarian directly in treatment. For instance, the patient with aphasia is not able to express his own thoughts, and he may have difficulty understanding the speech and writing of others. Much of this loss, usually acquired through an accident or stroke, can be recovered with speech therapy. The hospital library should contain a file of material which will assist in aphasia rehabilitation. Pictures which express one concept only, cards with one word, letter, or number to identify, and books with simple sentences in large print are all useful and permit involvement by the librarian. An aphasia kit containing just such picture and word cards and an instruction manual is available for use with aphasic patients.[3]

Not infrequently a hospital stay can lead either to follow-up treatment or to a chronic condition which means an altered way of life. The diabetic must learn a regimen of diet and medication; the tubercular patient must adjust to a long period of medication which must be meticulously followed, and he must learn to live by health rules that protect both himself and those who come in contact with him. Victims of heart attacks, strokes, and other physical disablements must learn to accept an altered way of life. In learning to understand and accept the physical problem, patients find that many of the related psychological problems diminish.

There are some patients to whom the nature of their illness is too traumatic to read about in cold print. For these persons individual counseling by their physician is advised, and an encounter revealing this problem should be reported to the head nurse.

Voluntary agencies and the U.S. Public Health Service have promoted many programs of education and health information, so that there is a great deal of authoritative material on every type of health problem. The hospital library should be the repository for staff-approved material, to be distributed on the advice of a staff member. The level of community health is raised by having a hygienically aware public. There is no question of the value of preventive medicine. Within the hospital, where patients are recuperating, the librarian should be concerned with reaching them prior to discharge. Proper information, often accompanied by instruction, will facilitate subsequent outpatient care. Health education for the improvement of outpatient care has been recommended by the working party of an American Hospital Association conference.[4]

Hospital routine and the patient's physical condition are not conducive to involvement in weighty affairs, so that scholarly or controversial materials are not recommended. For the physically disabled person talking books are now available, and there are many mechanical aids to assist readers who need these devices. Book cart service should be available to all stations, and ambulatory patients should be allowed to spend time in the patients' library.

Group bibliotherapy programs are not indicated for the average short-term patient, but much can be done, even during a short stay, to dispel the frustrations and apprehensions that occur, and to make the patient more aware of the need for healthful living.

The Physically Handicapped

The complex problems of the disabled individual have contributed to the development of a team approach in which the various disciplines focus

their combined attention on physical restoration and psychosocial rehabilitation. The chronically ill and disabled must learn to live within the limits
of their disability and, in addition, compensate for their loss by developing
to the full their other capacities. This is possible when the individual has
the support and guidance of a team which attacks the total problem.

Body image is a strong factor in personality, so that their physical defects
have a deep significance for disabled persons. They are confronted by two
basic psychological needs: the need for self-esteem and the need for high
evaluation by others. Moreover, they may be overprotected or rejected in
the home, there may be social rejection, or the individual may be discrimi-
nated against in seeking employment. Loss of mobility and economic problems cause further frustration. The disabled must learn, as Wright states,
that

> not all of life is influenced, let alone determined, by disability. The per-
> son with a disability must be encouraged to pinpoint the values now
> lost to him so that they become dots in the large map of the world, in
> which vast areas remain relatively intact and accessible. He will then
> realize that he is not a disabled person but a person with a disability,
> that life has a multitude of meanings, opportunities, and frustrations,
> only some of which are disability connected.[5]

In the process of rehabilitation the first step must be the acceptance of
the altered condition. Instead of becoming too dependent on the rehabilitation worker for making and carrying out plans, the individual must actively
participate; plans and decisions must include his opinions, and he must be
able to accept these decisions as real and valid. In discussing this aspect
of physical disability Siller writes:

> The goal of rehabilitation never changes—it is always directed to-
> ward promoting ego integrity and feelings of self-worth—but the spe-
> cific operations of the rehabilitation unit must constantly shift, being
> coordinated with the physical, psychological, and social realities of the
> rehabilitant. The danger arises when these operations are mistakenly
> identified as being the ultimate goal. Thus, one speaks of prosthetic
> rehabilitation, vocational rehabilitation, and so on, as entities in them-
> selves. It is my position that these are partial processes, the timing of
> which is governed by a strategy designed to foster the ego-integrative
> qualities of the rehabilitant.[6]

Guided reading can play a considerable part in restoring ego integrity.
By applying the principles of psychotherapy associated with reading, universalization, identification, catharsis, and insight, it is possible to resolve
many problems and frustrations during the period of counseling and retraining, provided the patient is able to achieve, through his own efforts or those

of his counselors, the understanding and motivation which lead to new attitudes. If significant reading material is provided at each step along the way, it may contribute to acceptance of the loss; stimulate active participation in the rehabilitative program; reinforce psychotherapeutic counseling; assist in retraining; and provide a recreational outlet as a substitute for physical activity. This will support the therapist and provide independent activity for the individual.

Library service to the handicapped has received increasing attention since 1966, when Title IV-B of the Library Services and Construction Act was passed. In addition, an amendment to the Library Services to the Blind Act allows the handicapped who cannot use conventional printed materials to borrow book recordings, tapes, and playback equipment. These have been important steps for the disabled, the chronically ill, and the elderly, in that they set in motion definite achievable plans, and make the state library agency responsible for utilizing and enlarging upon existing community resources. A general assessment of the development of these programs and an inventory of the number and kinds of people to be served are described by Graham, who states that, after thirty-five years in which federal and state vocational training and rehabilitation have existed, libraries are now being called upon to extend service to persons with special needs, not only to the physically handicapped but also to the economically depressed and the educationally handicapped.[7]

Since there are special schools and services for the deaf and the blind, these two groups will receive individual mention, although every type of disability has unique features that may require different techniques.

THE DEAF

Library service for the deaf child requires adjustments in book selection which take into account the language problems inherent in deafness. The child's development comes only from direct experiences, and there is great difficulty in acquiring language and communication skills when the child's experience has been meager. He must be able to coordinate what he sees in books and films with his own personal experiences, as this is the only link he has to abstract concepts.

The deaf child has no emotional attachment to books, so his first training must be with simple nature-study films, simple holiday films, or films about pets. These can be related to his personal life. The use of these films in the library provides vicarious experience, familiarizes the child with the location of the library, associates the library with a pleasurable experience, and provides a bridge from direct experience to films and then to books.

Picture books with large, simple, uncluttered illustrations are most suitable. Fairy tales are difficult for the deaf child to understand, as the language is strange and involved, and the child has no way of relating to the fanciful situation.

The deaf child is very dependent upon storytelling, since it provides an introduction to all kinds of literature, and becomes the basis for developing continued interest in reading. The difficulty and strain of lipreading requires intense concentration, and the deaf child's attention cannot be held as long as that of the hearing child. Independent reading of stories that have been told to him increases the child's skill as a reader. It is also necessary to use captioned films and filmstrips that are within the range of his vocabulary.

So that all media can be used more effectively, a greatly expanded program was made possible by the Captioned Films for the Deaf Act. (P.L. 89–258). This federal legislation was signed into law in 1965. It provides for the development and dissemination of material, training of personnel, and research dealing with the use of these materials.

The loss of sensory stimulation must be compensated for through reading. As noted in the *Standards for Library-Media Centers in Schools for the Deaf:*

> Deaf children miss the pleasurable sounds like jingles, nonsense words, or the cadence of rhymes that hearing children early associate in a pleasurable way with books as they are being read aloud to. They also miss any casually heard introduction to stories; they need to have the visual experience repeated many times.[8]

According to Levine, the lag which occurs in the development of the deaf can be compensated for by a longer period of training, since the deaf necessarily learn at a slower rate. She applies this to the emotional problems that may arise from this lag in stating:

> If an appellation were to be used, the term "underdeveloped" would be most appropriate, more to the point than "immaturity"; for "emotional immaturity" has come to be associated with psychotherapeutic needs, whereas "emotional under-development" implies that the basic needs lie rather in the area of education.[9]

By the time maturity is reached, reading interests and habits should be well established, so that the librarian's task is to supply material which will be informative and enjoyable, and which will enhance sensory and imaginative experience. This will help to keep the deaf person from feeling isolated from the mainstream of thought and action.

THE BLIND

Since 1931, when Congress voted its first appropriation for free distribution of material in Braille, service to the blind has had notable growth. Consistent support from governmental and voluntary agencies, good organization and administration of the program, and the development of electronic equipment have accounted for the wide distribution and great variety of material available to those who cannot use conventional printed matter.

Visual impairment and blindness are serious handicaps which affect scholastic, social, and vocational development. The total personality is altered, although the extent to which this occurs varies with the individual. The degree of sight, the cause of blindness, and the age of onset are all factors which influence the person in making an adequate adjustment to this sensory loss. One of the great disadvantages of impaired vision is that the individual cannot acquire behavior patterns by imitation based on visual observation, but must learn in more difficult ways how to conduct himself. The importance of the various media of communication which are open to him cannot be overemphasized.

The blind person does not automatically acquire greater sensitivity in order to compensate for his loss. He learns through trial and error to use his other faculties, and all of his other senses are constantly providing clues to which he responds. Lowenfeld notes three areas in which blindness changes or modifies the other senses: in experiencing the object world, in getting about, and in controlling the environment.[10]

The development of recording and playback equipment has made it possible for the blind to be educated in the community rather than in special schools. They may receive part of their training in special classes, but it is now felt that there is a great advantage in growing up in contact with seeing children, and in competing on as equal a footing as possible. In most modern public schools the child with impaired sight will have the advantage of special resources and teaching methods, his textbooks will be on tape or on records, and his recreational reading, borrowed from a library of talking books, will be the same stories every child enjoys.

The inclusion of the partially sighted and physically disabled in the service previously reserved for the legally blind has expanded the program immeasurably. The homebound reader, individuals and groups in nursing homes, and bedfast patients who may be incapacitated for a short or long period of time are all eligible. There are a number of mechanical aids which assist the reader, but many people, particularly the elderly, find it difficult to use these devices and prefer to rely on recorded materials. Graham presents a statistical analysis of the incidence and prevalence of the chronically ill and disabled who would benefit from participation in this service to the blind and physically handicapped, but feels they will need assistance in applying to the lending agency, and becoming familiar with the variety of material offered.[11] Reixach reviews the Library of Congress program and describes the extent of material available, including the way in which special needs are met through volunteer help in transcribing into Braille and onto tape any kind of information that is requested.[12] The article is followed by a listing of the centers where tapes, records, and books for the blind and handicapped may be obtained.[13]

Talking Book Topics and the *Braille Book Review* are published bimonthly to keep readers informed about recent releases. The American Foundation for the Blind prepares an annotated catalog which is sent to readers, and the Division of the Blind compiles a catalog of tape recordings, *Books on Magnetic Tape*. Talking-book machines are provided free to readers. Tape-recording cassettes are now replacing conventional tape recorders, and materials are being transcribed onto cassette tape.

There has been a concerted effort, both public and private, to increase the amount of material useful to those with impaired sight. Church denominations and other organizations offer recorded and large-print religious materials. Commercial producers supply recordings, large-print books, magazines, and newspapers. Mechanical reading aids are supplied by a number of manufacturers.

A service called Radio Talking Books is a recent innovation being offered to the visually handicapped by the Minnesota Services to the Blind; it is funded by the Hamm Foundation of St. Paul, Minnesota. A single-channel radio is supplied to each user. The daily broadcast schedule includes news; topics of local interest; programs that appeal to women listeners only and to men only; excerpts from current magazines; and regular talking-book materials.

Following the expansion of the Library of Congress program which was funded in 1966, a survey was initiated to determine the interests of present users and to chart future policies. A brief report of the survey, made by Nelson Associates, was published in *Talking Book Topics*.[14] At present 43 percent of the readers are 65 years old or older, and since reading needs and preferences are quite similar for adult readers, this presents few problems in the general selection of material to be recorded. However, the survey recommends that the collection strive for diversity, so that the interests of young and minority readers will be fully represented.

With current news sources, social comment, and general literature available to them, there is no reason for the handicapped to be isolated, but they do need help in being directed to those sources which will meet their needs.

The Mentally Ill

The term "bibliotherapy" has traditionally been associated with the mentally ill. When psychotherapy was restricted to classical analysis, bibliotherapy was viewed with disfavor by some therapists because it was a structured activity. Since that time psychotherapy has expanded in many directions to include any activity or device that will assist in the treatment of the mentally ill.

Therapeutic library services fall within the range of several present-day methods of therapy for the mentally ill. One is milieu therapy, which is defined by Folsom as "the beneficial effects of proper hospital atmosphere, routine, and personnel structure. More specifically, Milieu Therapy is the psychiatric treatment of mental disorder through the use of prescribed adjustments in the environment so as to meet the unconscious needs of the individual and direct the personality back to its normal course of development."[15]

Reality therapy is another break with tradition, one in which reading offers strong support. It is based on the premise that the individual must take responsibility for his own behavior; he must accept the reality of the situation in which he finds himself, and distinguish right action from wrong. In this he needs the support of some person who genuinely cares about his welfare and whose opinion he values, so that through this relationship he gains involvement and fulfills his needs. As Glasser explains, the therapist maintains an attitude of love and concern for the patient while at the same time demanding responsible behavior, and never condoning irresponsible behavior.[16]

Rome believes that with the use of drugs psychiatric patients become amenable to modified versions of treatment, and can be helped to an improved level of adaptation through some kind of educational process.[17] One treatment method of this kind, on an elementary level, is remotivation technique. It is designed to stimulate the patient's interest in a variety of subjects, to rekindle his intellectual curiosity, and to focus his attention on the workaday world to which he will return. The library is an important resource for the remotivation group leader in choosing material to present to the group, and it can provide additional reading material on a subject that may turn out to be of particular interest to a patient. Remotivation technique can be modified to fit all categories of patients, but the basic structure remains the same.[18]

Kinney describes a method of group bibliotherapy which is conducted by the librarian. She notes that it is important to set a goal in advance, and to keep a regular schedule of sessions, as progress is slow and the effort must be sustained over a considerable period of time to show conclusive results.[19]

The bibliotherapy project developed as part of the Title IV program at Agnews State Hospital, California, consists of sessions held twice a day, four days a week, in the library. In the beginning the therapist was a physician working in conjunction with the librarian, who was the resource person for the project. Some recorded materials were used. In the final report the comments of professional staff observers are included. One comment, quoted in part, sums up the value of successful bibliotherapy with the mentally ill:

> A general tendency in therapy is the constant effort to focus on the individual's personal and immediate life experiences and his attitudes about society, morals, religion, mankind, politics—*Weltanschauung*—are often discarded as rationalizations, intellectualizations, and clouding and coloring of the "basic" problems. While this may be so, it is still evident that those general views and values play an important role in the patient's mental and emotional world. We witness this in various paranoid delusional systems; in the pessimistic outlook of the depressed; in various complaints and social criticisms of young addicts. It is noticed also in various stages of therapy when the patient struggles with reevaluating previous mistaken, distorted, or other concepts which had interfered with his ability to function and cope with arising problems. In the bibliotherapy sessions I could observe an opposite trend in which discussions of the general values and opinions carried over and helped solve very personal problems. There is not enough evidence yet as to what new possibilities and therapeutic avenues this approach may bring about. Yet, even the limited experience in recent sessions held great promise.[20]

There is a definite tendency among depressed and schizophrenic patients to lose interest in reading. Favazza's study of 25 psychiatric and 18 matched medical control patients bears this out. Shifts in individual reading patterns have diagnostic value, and should be noted. In group bibliotherapy the patient need not make a conscious effort to read and absorb the printed matter. During certain phases of his illness he may remain passive, listening to the reading, commenting when stirred by the discussion, or responding only when he is prompted by the leader or by some member of the group.[21]

Many patients are now confined to mental hospitals for fairly short periods of time, returning to their homes to continue treatment at a community mental health center. It is hoped that at some future date hospitals which successfully use bibliotherapy in their treatment programs will arrange to continue this activity through community libraries or mental health centers.

Bibliotherapy session,
Agnews State Hospital,
San Jose, California

The Mentally Retarded

The American Association of Mental Deficiency defines mental retardation as "subaverage general intellectual functioning which originates during the developmental period and is associated with impairment in adaptive behavior."[22] Perlstein modifies this definition by stating that "mental retardation is defined as a group of syndromes occurring before the completion of growth and development, and characterized by reduced intellectual capacity to a point of impaired learning ability and social inadequacy." He also makes this observation:

The difference between a mentally retarded and a normal child tends to become more obvious with age up to about 15 or 16 years. After this age, barring irreversible bad habits, the manifest differences usually decrease. At age 25 to 30 years, the difference between a mentally retarded and a normal person may be much less apparent than it was at age 12. . . . In adult life, the world cares little how smart one was at school, but pays much more attention to how one behaves.[23]

Perlstein classifies the educability of the retarded as follows:

The Totally Dependent
  I.Q. below 25. These children are incapable of being trained for total self-care. They develop at about one-fourth the rate of average children, and cannot care for their personal needs or communicate effectively with others. These individuals require custodial care.

The Trainable Child
  I.Q. 25 to 50. These children can usually acquire basic skills of living, and many of them can attain a primary level of education. They can be trained in social behavior and conduct themselves adequately at home and in the community. They may be capable of work experience in a sheltered workshop.

The Educable Child
  I.Q. 50 to 75. This group is the responsibility of the community rather than of an institution. They are educated in public schools, or in special schools where the emphasis is on learning through activity rather than through abstract methods.[24]

Present-day methods of teaching the mentally retarded are raising the level of accomplishment of these individuals. The main objectives in their education are self-realization, good human relationships, economic self-sufficiency, and civic responsibility. The mental age which is obtained through standard testing methods is not a true indication of the individual's ability. Gunsburg has compared a normal child aged 5 years and 5 months and a mentally handicapped youth 18 years old, whose mental age is also 5 years and 5 months. Although retarded, the 18-year-old has acquired many social achievements that are beyond the capacity of the 5-year-old.[25] Social development is very uneven, and each person's social skills must be rated individually. Gunsburg summarizes:

> It has been shown that the social functioning of the subnormal can be well above the level indicated by the test of mental ability. The discrepancy can be very large if good education and maturation have contributed to an advanced degree of social competence.[26]

He further states that the real problem in training the retarded is their lack of a desire to learn and their inability to strive toward a goal. The subnormal displays a marked degree of passive acceptance of his handicap, and will do little to overcome his shortcoming. This is understandable when one considers the lack of success the retarded have experienced as compared with their normal peers.

The objectives of library service for the retarded stress support for educational and social gains, with the added objective of stimulating the enjoyment of reading as a leisure-time activity. Library programs should reinforce and supplement in a relaxed, less structured way the regular school curriculum, and there are many library activities which can provide opportunities for the child to experience success, thereby stimulating a desire for further achievement. The wide range of low-vocabulary, high-interest materials now being published do not condemn the older retardate to reading "little kid's" books. The library should be well equipped with audiovisual materials, with basic sight vocabulary materials, and with games and objects which can be incorporated into group or individual free-time activities.

In recent years the religious needs of the retarded have received particular attention, and an annotated list of material on the subject of mental retardation and religion has been published in *Mental Retardation Abstracts*.[27] Youth organizations such as Boy Scouts, Girl Scouts, Campfire Girls, and 4-H clubs have published plans for activities with groups of the retarded. Other organizations are showing similar concern, so that lack of academic achievement need not bar the retarded from religious or social activities. Nor should it bar them from becoming regular users of the library.

The Offender

Crime is defined as an act forbidden by law, and punishable upon conviction. The causes are numerous, and there is no one way of describing them. According to the report of the President's Commission on Law Enforcement and Administration of Justice, there are more than 2,800 federal crimes and a much larger number of state and local ones. Public expenditures for the police, courts, and corrections are estimated by the report at $4 billion a year.[28]

A composite picture drawn from a number of sources indicates that although offenders themselves differ strikingly, certain characteristics predominate: the great majority are male; most are young, ranging in age between 16 and 30; a high proportion are handicapped educationally, and many have dropped out of school. Offenders tend to have unstable work records, a large proportion coming from backgrounds of poverty so that material failure is the most common denominator; many, too, have failed in their relationships with family and friends. Whether adult or juvenile, they have little self-esteem, and are, in fact, chronic losers in the game of life.

Reflecting public and official concern over this ever-growing sociological problem, the 89th Congress passed three major bills: the Law Enforcement Act, the Correctional Rehabilitation Study Act, and the Prisoner Rehabilitation Act, all aimed at the prevention of crime and the rehabilitation of public offenders.[29]

The National Inventory of Library Needs included an inventory of library resources in correctional institutions, which was compiled by the American Correctional Association and AHIL.[30] The results of the survey indicate that the lack of adequate resources and trained personnel in institution libraries is hampering efforts to train and rehabilitate prison inmates. According to Vedder:

> The library shares in common with other units or divisions of the institution the responsibility for educational, social, recreational, and vocational training of the people committed to the institution. In carrying out this function, the library program:
>
> 1. Provides vocational information
> 2. Enlarges social and reading backgrounds
> 3. Develops reading as a satisfying leisure-time activity, a therapeutic release from strain, and a positive aid in substituting new interests for undesirable attitudes
> 4. Prepares the individual, through his own efforts, for release and post-prison life.[31]

The section of the *Manual of Correctional Standards* that has to do with library services presents the basic essentials of a correctional institution library.[32] The library which conforms to these standards fulfills an important function in the life of the offender, since it provides a constructive area within the institution that has a counterpart in the outside world. Too many prison libraries, however, are merely marginal adjuncts in the institution. Attempts are being made to demonstrate the true value of attractive libraries, professionally and intelligently administered, offering a motivating and enjoyable collection of material to the many types of readers found in a correctional institution. Title IV-A of LSCA has provided funds for upgrading facilities and collections, but existing facilities were so meager when the program was initiated that long-term, sustained efforts will be needed.

Present-day thinking in regard to prison libraries tends toward creating an attractive environment that is in marked contrast to the rest of the institution, so that the physical surroundings will stimulate and challenge the reader. Open stacks, inviting reading and browsing areas, programmed learning and audiovisual aids, a conference room for group sessions, and special collections on vocational guidance, family relationships, and the general conduct of life are all important in providing adequate library service. In addition to meeting the needs of the inmates, the resources of the library should be available to the correctional staff.

Group activities offered in prisons include Alcoholics Anonymous, Dale Carnegie courses, formal education, sports, and group therapy with a counselor, chaplain, social worker, or volunteer. Great Books programs have been successful but do not reach all levels of inmates, so that many other kinds of reading programs should be devised to reach those with less interest or intelligence, or reading should be used in conjunction with other therapeutic activities. By reinforcing group activity with individual reading, the inmate develops his own resources instead of constantly relying on the help of others.

The therapist in a correctional institution has the responsibility of reaching the inmate at his level of comprehension and motivating him to acquire attitudes that will lead to behavior change. The inmate has the responsibility of recognizing his need, cooperating in a sustained program of training and therapy, and assuming the burden of his own rehabilitation. The librarian has the responsibility of choosing materials which will be an adequate resource for many kinds of therapists and many levels of intelligence among the prisoners, and for developing library programs which will fill a wide spectrum of needs. Regardless of the librarian's views on book selection, the choice of material must conform to the institution's policies and philosophies.

Efforts at preventing crime are directed mainly toward children and youth. Since our system of justice holds both juveniles and adults responsible for their misconduct, "society thereby obligates itself to equip juveniles with the means—the educational and social and cultural background, the personal and economic security—to understand and accept responsibility," as stated in the report of the President's Commission.[33]

Since the young offender is still of school age, his education is of primary importance. In many cases home influences and those of peer groups may be so difficult to overcome that the child needs a great deal of counseling before learning can be effective.

The difference between therapy and education is described in a research study by Roman, entitled *Reaching Delinquents through Reading.* He states, "All forms of therapy attempt to create a setting in which patients can have helpful new experiences and learn from them, the basic objective is to bring about corrective emotional experiences." He explains that therapy directs itself to the deviant aspects of personality, the symptoms of character disturbance, with a view to effecting change in the individual pathology. In contrasting this with education, Roman continues:

> Education, on the other hand, directs itself to those functions of the ego undisturbed by conflict. It requires the ability to judge, to learn by experience, to gain understanding and to plan. While education and psychotherapy are basically dissimilar, educational experience can and very often does have therapeutic effects . . . similarly, a therapeutic experience can result in educational gains.[34]

In his research study Roman integrated psychotherapy and remedial reading into what he calls "tutorial group therapy." The group was told that they were not going to be taught to read, but rather to discover what had interfered with their ability to read. They were free to use the meetings to talk or read, as they wished. In reading remedial techniques were used; in talk sessions the meetings were conducted along therapeutic lines, with the reading process used as a means of stimulating discussion.[35] The results, which were thoroughly tested, indicate that this technique is more effective than either group remedial reading or interview group therapy in treating delinquent children who present a reading disability in conjunction with emotional disturbance.

In *Hooked on Books* Fader reports on a different type of project. This was not a selective reading program, but rather the exposure of institutionalized delinquent boys to all kinds of literature through a free choice of paperback books, together with the use of newspapers and magazines in classrooms. Every class was used to develop facility in basic communicative skills, and any therapeutic results were incidental.[36] Dr. Fader's plan has had marked success in a variety of settings, and has opened the way for a more liberal use of many kinds of current materials which have relevance for disadvantaged and minority groups.

Libraries, as well as educational systems, must create the kinds of service that will appeal to all races and all strata of society, so that everyone may come to understand the need for a sense of personal responsibility and of just treatment of others. During a time of rapid social change new patterns of culture emerge, and all individuals and racial and ethnic groups must learn to understand and adapt to these changes.

Alcoholics and Narcotic Addicts

Addiction in all its forms has become a rapidly expanding problem, and at present it touches all age groups and social strata. The situation is compounded by the divergence of opinions regarding causes and cures. Is addiction a physical illness, or is it a mental disease? Is the addict legally and morally responsible for his behavior, or should his addiction absolve him from blame for acts committed under the influence of drugs or alcohol? Should addiction be regarded as a medical, legal, moral, or educational problem?

The disease concept of alcoholism is now accepted to the point where the alcoholic in many cases is treated as any other patient with a physical ailment. Mann defines alcoholism as "a disease which manifests itself chiefly by the uncontrollable drinking of the victim."[37] She believes that the alcoholic has lost the power of choice in the matter of drinking. Szasz, on the other hand, stresses the issue of choice and freedom in the use of alcohol. He disputes the concept of alcoholism as a disease by saying that people do not voluntarily choose cancer or heart disease, but that they do choose to drink.[38]

The individual voluntarily joins groups such as Alcoholics Anonymous and Synanon as a means of keeping his addiction under control, and becomes motivated to lend his support to the other members of his group. Support is offered at many levels, psychological, educational, religious, and recreational. Whatever the need of the individual at a critical moment, the members of the group will rally to provide it. Formal rehabilitation programs with client-therapist relationships seldom achieve the success of programs in which strong supportive measures are provided by the group members for one another. Rusalem points out:

As formal rehabilitation programs open their doors wider to narcotics addicts, rehabilitation workers are confronted by the reality that members of this disability group do not usually adapt well to traditional measures. Rehabilitation technics that require high levels of client motivation and cooperation, demand consistency of performance, and assume a universal drive for health, survival, and self improvement often achieve minimal results with the addict. Emotionally fragile, alienated from middle-class values, and unresponsive to many counseling procedure, the addict seems to reject the interventions that have worked so well with other disability groups.[39]

There have been accounts of discussion groups based on reading in institutions, in halfway houses, and in community therapy groups, but there are no definitive methods or materials other than the Alcoholics Anonymous books and the instructional materials used in school curricula.

One therapy group which met in a library has been described by Dr. Richard O. Heilman, chief of the Alcohol Unit, Department of Psychiatry, Veterans Administration Hospital, Minneapolis, Minnesota. Dr. Heilman chose the library as a meeting place because he felt the atmosphere was good, and that the library had a psychological impact. He describes the alcoholic as one whose purpose in life is lost, whose goals have become vague. He will be passive, depressed, and lacking in self-esteem. He has difficulty accepting other people's opinions and ideas, but will accept the authority of the printed word. Books by doctors, psychologists, sociologists, theologians, lay people, and recovered alcoholics will be accepted. Dr. Heilman believes that many programs are too passive, but that reading programs give involvement. The patients must read and report on books, and even the responsibility of checking out and returning books on time is a positive activity. The world of ideas which is opened to these patients through their reading will counteract the negative state of mind which is so prevalent with persons under treatment for alcoholism. The fear, depression, or illness which result from drinking will not bring the patient to sobriety; he must have positive reasons for making the effort, and in their reading and discussions the patients do find alternatives, and develop a facility for communication which strengthens positive attitudes.[40]

The epidemic proportions of drug use among the young has stimulated a great deal of research as to how to understand and deal with the problem. The complexities of modern society, as well as disillusionment with it, and weakened family structures have contributed to the insecurity of the young. King describes the problems of young people as an effect of modern living, a form of narcissism in which youth react to life by rebellion or by withdrawal. He says:

> Drugs provide one avenue for withdrawal, whether into oblivion with heroin, or the mind-blown world with LSD, or the speeded-up experience with amphetamines. A type of withdrawal also occurs with "pot" in which reaction time becomes retarded and life seems to stand still. Drugs represent one way of responding to crisis. The danger lies in abrogating the task of maturing in a rapidly changing society for which there is no blueprint providing safe guidelines into the future."[41]

Preventive measures are the responsibility of parents, the schools, and the churches, which provide religious influences to which the young person may respond. When treatment and rehabilitation are necessary, the psychiatric team and the ancillary therapies become involved. The problem is too serious to omit any service which may be helpful, and institution and community libraries should be called upon to contribute their resources. Librarians must be trained to encourage purposeful reading and participation in discussion groups so that rapport within the group will be strengthened, and the members will mutually help one another to develop attitudes of self-worth and an adequate value system.

Notes

1. Hans Mauksch, Co/Ordinated Communications, Inc., *Pulse on Patient Relations* 1:4 (Dec. 1962).
2. F. J. Kottke, "Deterioration of the Bedfast Patient," *Public Health Reports* 80:437–51 (May 1965).
3. M. L. Taylor and M. M. Marks, *Aphasia: Rehabilitation Manual and Therapy Kit* (New York: McGraw-Hill, 1955).
4. American Hospital Association, *Outpatient Health Care* (Chicago: The Association, 1969), p.26.
5. B. A. Wright, *Physical Disability—A Psychological Approach* (New York: Harper, 1960), p.128.
6. J. Siller, "Psychological Situation of the Disabled with Spinal Cord Injuries," *Rehabilitation Literature* 30:290–96 (Oct. 1969).
7. E. C. Graham, "Public Library Services to the Handicapped," *ALA Bulletin* 61:170–79 (Feb. 1967).
8. U.S. Office of Education, *Standards for Library-Media Centers in Schools for the Deaf* (Washington, D.C.: Govt. Print. Off., 1967), p.10–11.
9. E. S. Levine, "The Deaf," in J. F. Garrett, ed., *Psychological Aspects of Physical Disability* (U.S. Office of Vocational Rehabilitation, Rehabilitation Series no.210 [Washington, D.C.: Govt. Print. Off.]), p.125–46.
10. Berthold Lowenfeld, "The Blind," in J. F. Garrett, ed., *Psychological Aspects of Physical Disability,* p.179–95.
11. Graham, "Public Library Services to the Handicapped," p.171–72.
12. K. Reixach, "Talking Books Bridge the Communication Gap for Blind and Handicapped Patients," *Modern Nursing Home* 23:77–78 (July–Aug. 1969).
13. "Tapes, Records, Books for the Blind and Handicapped Offered by These Centers," *Modern Nursing Home* 23:79–80 (July–Aug. 1969).
14. Library of Congress, Division of the Blind and Physically Handicapped, "Report of the Nelson Survey," *Talking Book Topics* 35:147 (Sept. 1969).
15. J. C. Folsom, "Attitude Therapy as a Communication Device," *Transactions* (Department of Psychiatry, Marquette School of Medicine) 1:18–26 (Spring 1969).
16. William Glasser, *Reality Therapy: A New Approach to Psychiatry* (New York: Harper, 1965), p.1–41.
17. H. P. Rome, "Whence, Whither and Why: Psychiatry, Circa 1964," in W. K. Beatty, ed., "Proceedings of the ALA Bibliotherapy Workshop, St. Louis, June 25–27, 1964," *AHIL Quarterly* 4:31–40 (Summer 1964).
18. A. M. Robinson, *Remotivation Technique* (Philadelphia: Smith, Kline and French Laboratories Remotivation Project 1959).

19. M. M. Kinney, "The Patients' Library in a Psychiatric Setting," *AHIL Quarterly* 6:12–17 (Winter 1966).

20. E. Steffens, "Agnews State Hospital Patients Library Bibliotherapy Project (1968–1969)" (unpublished report, Project #3692, Title IV-A).

21. A. R. Favazza, "Shifts of Reading Pattern as a Diagnostic Tool in Psychiatric Patients," *Diseases of the Nervous System* 28:589–92 (Sept. 1967).

22. R. Heber, "Modifications in the Manual on Terminology and Classification in Mental Retardation," *American Journal of Mental Deficiency* 65:499–500 (Jan. 1961).

23. M. A. Perlstein, "The Nature and Classification of Mental Deficiency," *World-Wide Abstracts of General Medicine* 8:16–28 (May 1965).

24. Ibid., p.18–20.

25. H. C. Gunsburg, *Social Competence and Mental Handicap* (London, Eng.: Baillière, Tindall and Cassell, 1968), p.19.

26. Ibid., p.20.

27. J. S. Snodgrass, "Mental Retardation and Religion (An Annotated Bibliography)," *Mental Retardation Abstracts* 3:502–8 (Oct.–Dec. 1966).

28. President's Commission on Law Enforcement and Administration of Justice, *The Challenge of Crime in a Free Society* (Washington, D.C.: Govt. Print. Off., 1967), p.17–53.

29. G. E. Ayers and C. R. Weber, "Contemporary Problems in Community Acceptance of the Public Offender," *Rehabilitation Literature* 28:374–76, 382 (Dec. 1967).

30. American Correctional Association and Association of Hospital and Institution Libraries, "Inventory of Library Resources in Correctional Institutions," in *National Inventory of Library Needs* (Chicago: American Library Assn., 1965).

31. M. H. Vedder, "Position Paper on Correctional Institution Libraries," *AHIL Quarterly* 9:18–21 (Fall 1968).

32. Committee on Institutional Libraries, "Library Services," in American Correctional Association, *Manual of Correctional Standards* (3d ed.; Washington, D.C.: The Association, 1966), p.502–18.

33. President's Commission on Law Enforcement and Administration of Justice, *The Challenge of Crime in a Free Society*, p.58.

34. M. Roman, *Reaching Delinquents through Reading* (Springfield, Ill.: Thomas, 1957), p.100–1.

35. Ibid., p.103.

36. D. N. Fader and E. B. McNeil, *Hooked on Books: Program and Proof* (New York: Berkley, 1968).

37. M. Mann, *Primer on Alcoholism* (New York: Holt, 1950), p.3.

38. T. S. Szasz, "Alcoholism: A Socio-ethical Perspective," *Transactions* (Department of Psychiatry, Marquette School of Medicine) 1:7–12 (Spring 1969).

39. H. Rusalem, "A Capsule Research Review," *Rehabilitation Literature* v.29 (inside front cover) (May 1968).

40. R. O. Heilman, Unpublished paper presented at the 19th Mental Hospital Institute, Minneapolis, 25–28 Sept. 1967.

41. S. H. King, "Youth in Rebellion: An Historical Perspective," in *Drug Dependence* (Chevy Chase, Md.: National Institute of Mental Health), July 1969, p.5–9.

Methods
and
Materials

Resources of the Library in Therapy

The institution library collection must first of all reflect the interests and needs of the general reader; in this respect it resembles a small public library collection. Secondly, it should supplement the institution's formal educational program and, thirdly, it should be an ample and innovative resource for the variety of activities carried out by the ancillary therapies. Institutional librarianship is also an ancillary therapy, advanced by a diversified collection of resources. The librarian's work rests upon his utilization of available materials. As noted in *Institutional Library Services: A Plan for the State of Illinois:*

> the librarian . . . must develop a role model so that . . . professional people regard him as one who can be a resource and a support for the achievement of the institution's goals. The librarian, therefore, must become a resource to staff in developing materials, planning material related to group development, group remotivation, and group therapy, as well as participate as a team member in individual treatment designs and educational programs.[1]

The scope of the general collection may be enlarged by a variety of nonbook materials and by mechanical reading aids. In some institutions the use of audiovisual materials is so extensive that a separate department is maintained for storing and repairing equipment and for loaning materials. However, reading aids and nonprint materials which are for library use only should be part of the library inventory.

Ephemeral materials find many uses in therapy, particularly in remotivation technique and similar programs. With the retarded many kinds of objects are useful: posters, poetry, pictures, maps, clippings, pamphlets, hand puppets, and lists of objects with notations giving the source from which the materials may be obtained. These files will save the therapy staff a great deal of time and effort, but they must be kept up to date, and be weeded often enough to eliminate material which is no longer current. Maintenance of these files may be the work of a volunteer or of a patient or resident assigned to library duty.

Fiction is widely used in bibliotherapy because it mirrors life situations. There are many publications with classified and annotated lists which will save the therapist's time in locating suitable material. These lists should be checked to indicate which items are available in the library.

Nonfiction materials which will be useful in other therapy programs include arts and crafts, games, sports, short skits and plays, song books, suggestions for parties, and the celebration of holidays. For personal and social development materials on home economics, building and home repairs, personal hygiene and preventive medicine, popular psychology and self-help books, and etiquette and good grooming will be useful. Various editions of the Bible, including those in large print and in foreign languages, will also be needed. Bible reference materials will have limited use, and those on the general aspects of Christian and non-Christian religions will be more used than those dealing with doctrinal theology. Libraries are apt to be used to proselytize, so that gifts of religious material should be reviewed carefully before being added to the collection.

Books which deal with ethnic and racial cultures should be found in the collection, and material on current history and social problems should be available through clippings from newspapers and magazines. Home-town newspapers may be donated by the publisher upon request, or obtained through a local service organization.

Prison libraries should provide a good selection of materials on personal and social development and vocational guidance. It is also recommended that law books be provided for prisoners to use in working on their appeals for parole. The inmates should be encouraged to build their own collections of paperback reference books.

The librarian must be fully aware of the kinds of activities that are being planned, so that the needs will be met before, not after, program changes take place.

Library Group Activities

In planning library group activities which are not strictly bibliotherapy, the composition of the group is important since there must be a similarity of interests and needs. There can be many variations of the same type of activity, depending upon the age of the participants, their educational and cultural level, and the reason for including them in a particular group. In planning a series of sessions, a definite goal should be set so that the progress of each individual can be measured and recorded.

When the emphasis is on developmental and educational needs, excellent sources for choosing combinations of books, audiovisual aids, and other materials are the curriculum guides compiled by special education authorities. These are generally in the field of the educable mentally retarded or in that of basic adult education, but they are applicable to many situations. An outstanding example of this type of publication is *The Illinois Plan for Special Education of Exceptional Children: A Curriculum Guide for Teachers of the Educable Mentally Handicapped.*[2] This plan deals with life functions such as home and family, health and safety, money management, and social adjustment. It also covers academic areas of knowledge such as language arts, arithmetic, and science.

Gazda and others have indicated that groups may be formed according to the approach each individual may profit by, whether psychodrama, counseling, behavior modification, or psychoanalysis.[3] In other groups the intent may be to prepare the patients for or to supplement psychotherapy. The three-step plan of bibliotherapy described by Penny is a very basic form of therapeutic reading and discussion.[4] Many library groups are planned simply as pleasurable experiences in which enjoyment and enrichment are the principal goals.

The following are examples of activity therapy which use the resources of the library, and about which the librarian must be knowledgeable. There are also examples of activity therapy which take place in the library, and are planned and executed by the library staff.

MANNERS AND GROOMING

PURPOSE: To present a developmental program on manners, courtesy, and grooming for retarded or disadvantaged youth as a means of building self-awareness, confidence, and poise; to observe the group's ability to respond to factual learning, attitudinal learning, and concept learning.[5]

METHOD: This group meets in the library to supplement and reinforce classroom instruction. Audiovisual materials only are used, although books and articles clipped from magazines are recommended for individual reading. Each film or filmstrip is viewed twice, with a period of discussion in between. Factual learning is then tested. When it is determined that the facts presented are known, attitudinal questioning will bring out individual opinions of the subject matter. In concept learning the group should be able to generalize in fairly abstract terms the personal attitudes members have formed to the facts presented in the films.

MATERIALS: The material listed below on the subject of etiquette is typical of the kind of films to be used in the entire series:

Everyday Courtesy, Coronet Films (intermediate and advanced)
Mind Your Manners, Coronet Films (advanced)
Manners Make a Difference, Filmstrip House (advanced).

WHO'S WHO CLUB

PURPOSE: This is an institutional group which meets in the library for the purpose of increasing understanding and appreciation of the contribution that all ethnic and nationality groups make to our national life. It should also increase self-awareness and self-esteem, as each member represents a different group.

METHOD: Each session is devoted to one national or racial topic. The group member representing the subject under discussion acts as host and program planner. The program may include a talk by the host bringing out interesting historical and biographical facts about the race or nationality being studied. Pictures, filmstrips, or films may be used. A folk song or other typical music may be played, and there may be a display of arts and crafts. All members of the club are asked to bring a news item or picture relating to the subject for the day that would be suitable for an exhibit. These materials are assembled and kept in the library until the next meeting, when a new exhibit is made.

MATERIALS: Before the sessions get underway, the librarian should collect files of clippings, maps, pictures, or objects such as small flags for the participants to use. The resources of the community should be explored for arts and crafts which may be borrowed for the occasion. The person planning the program will need guidance in finding historical and biographical material, and will need printed or typed captions for the exhibit. A small shelf of books should accompany the exhibit. The following titles are typical:

Getting to Know Books (several series devoted to countries on all continents). Coward-McCann. Grades 3–5
Lives to Remember Biographies. Putnam. Grades 6–7
Americans All, Garrard. Grade 4.

CHORAL SPEAKING

PURPOSE: To improve articulation and expression in pupils or patients who have speech difficulties; may also be used as a general group activity.

METHOD: Practice includes techniques similar to those used in rehearsing singing groups. This activity may be used with all age groups, depending on the material chosen, and is a change from the usual speech drills. At the start choral-speaking records and tapes should be used, and later any poetry or prose that adapts well to being performed may be used. When the group becomes proficient, it may appear at assemblies or on institutional programs.

MATERIALS:

Choral Speaking for Primary Grades. Burgess Publishing Co., Minneapolis.

Choral Speaking for Intermediate Grades. Burgess Publishing Co.

Let's Say Poetry Together: A Record of Choral Speaking. Activity Records, Inc., Freeport, N.Y.

MODIFIED PSYCHODRAMA

PURPOSE: To develop the ability to interact in situations by using prepared material with dialogue. These sessions may be used as preparation for true psychodrama. This is a good activity for recording on videotape and for playback discussion.

METHOD: Since there is little or no published material that is suitable for a dialogue of two or three minutes' duration, it will be necessary for the therapist to improvise. Some of the Sunday comic pages and some comic books contain material that will prove suitable. Participants assume the characters and play out the story. When this can be done with ease, scripts of similar length based on familiar sayings, slogans, proverbs, or fables are prepared. The participants should practice reversing roles, since this is a common practice in psychodrama.

MATERIALS: As stated, there is little or no prepared material, but in addition to improvised material, excerpts from plays may be read. Scenes which will be within the capability of the group to read and understand are chosen.

MOTHERS' CLUB

PURPOSE: To facilitate re-entry of the mother into the family group upon discharge from an institution, to help build a close family relationship, and to provide a means for family recreation and socialization. This group is referred and counseled by a social worker.

METHOD: A group of women patients who have young children in the home are referred to the librarian for group activity. A variety of children's literature is available for browsing through. Each member chooses books and magazines which she feels would appeal to her child, and excerpts are read aloud. The librarian demonstrates storytelling, and television programs for children are discussed. Use of the public library for all the family is explained, and a visit to a public library is arranged. If the discussion leads to psychological problems which the mothers have in dealing with their children, these should be referred to the social worker.

MATERIALS: An attractive variety of children's books and magazines, and books on storytelling. The following are suggested:

Sechrist. *It's Time for Story Hour*. Grades 1–5. Macrae Smith

Carlson. *Listen and Help Tell the Story*. Grade K–2. Abingdon

Barrett. *Story Telling, It's Easy* (paper). Grades 1–6. Zondervan

Eakin, ed. *Good Books for Children*, 3d ed. University of Chicago Press.

GERIATRIC PERSONAL INTERVIEWS

PURPOSE: To sustain self-esteem in the elderly by having them record on tape interesting and important events in their lives; to make these recordings available to others who have similar interests.

METHOD: The subject is interviewed prior to taping to develop the most interesting points in the story. The recorded interview may use one or more questioners, and take place in private or with an audience. The tape is placed on file for replay to groups or for individual listeners to enjoy. Historical events, dramatic personal experiences, or humorous anecdotes in which the speaker played a part make good subjects. Recordings in foreign languages are enjoyed particularly by others of the same nationality. The tapes should be placed on file with complete notations about the interview.

MATERIALS: A good recorder, tape, and storage area are required. Cassette machines, which are available through the Title IV-B program, are very easy to transport and use. Fairly detailed data should be on file describing the taped interview.

DISCOVERY CLUB

PURPOSE: To provide an opportunity for institutionalized persons to become aware of interesting events happening in the outside world, and to participate as far as possible in these events. Current social problems, exceptional events such as space travel, or any noteworthy local news event may be the focus for discussion. This may be adapted to any age or interest level.

METHOD: The meetings are organized on a structure similar to that of remotivation technique, but without reference to vocational aspects. Topics may be planned to occupy more than one session. The members of the group gather their own material, but the use of an occasional outside speaker or a film of background interest will add variety. The preparation of an exhibit or scrapbook may help to sustain interest, and the group may wish to watch a related event on television together. Books and other reading material should be available for those who wish to pursue further study.

MATERIALS: Newspapers and current magazines will provide most of the material, and copies which can be clipped should be on hand. Reference materials such as atlases or encyclopedias will add depth.

ORIENTATION TO PSYCHOTHERAPY

PURPOSE: To provide newly hospitalized patients with orientation to the treatment program of the hospital, and prepare them for psychotherapy through a series of reading programs.

METHOD: Using mental health materials prepared for lay audiences, with emphasis on the informative rather than the therapeutic aspects of the program, the individual becomes familiar with the terminology of treatment and the various types of therapy used in the institution. The material to be used and the participants are chosen by the psychiatric team. The library is suggested as a neutral, nonclinical setting in which to orient the apprehensive new patient. Therapeutic problems which arise should be noted and referred to a member of the psychiatric team.

MATERIALS: Books, films, pamphlets, and clippings from periodicals should be approved by an appropriate staff member before being used with the patient or the group. The following are suggested for use:

Stern. *Mental Illness: A Guide for the Family,* rev. ed. Harper, 1957

Menninger and Leaf. *You and Psychiatry.* Scribner, 1968

Film. *How Are You?* Animated cartoon, color, 16 min. Medical Services, Minnesota Dept. of Public Welfare, 1966

Film. *People Who Care.* 25 min. National Association for Mental Health, 1955.

MAGAZINE CLUB

PURPOSE: To stimulate interest in cultural and current topics; to develop a facility for exchanging ideas about present-day activities which will keep the members of the group in touch with the outside world.

METHOD: After a general discussion of the purpose, contents, variety, and makeup of magazines, the issues which are currently received are displayed for perusal by the group. Choices are then made of those which each person would like to review regularly. Comments may be made on anything that catches the reviewer's interest, such as pictorial displays, stories, articles, advertising, poetry, or cartoons.

MATERIALS: Current issues of a wide variety of popular magazines should be available for making selections for review. Subsequent issues should be reserved for each reviewer so that they may be read and commented upon before being circulated.

Notes

1. Social, Educational Research and Development, Inc., *Institutional Library Services: A Plan for the State of Illinois* (Chicago: American Library Assn., 1970), p.49.

2. Herbert Goldstein, dir. and comp., *The Illinois Plan for Special Education of Exceptional Children: A Curriculum Guide for Teachers of the Educable Mentally Handicapped* (Danville, Ill.: Interstate Printers and Publishers, n.d.). 267p.

3. G. M. Gazda, ed., *Basic Approaches to Group Psychotherapy and Group Counseling* (Springfield, Ill.: Thomas, 1968), p.ix.

4. Ruthanna Penny, *Practical Care of the Mentally Retarded and Mentally Ill* (Springfield, Ill.: Thomas, 1966), p.171–76.

5. J. Driscoll, "Educational Films and the Slow Learner," *Mental Retardation* 6:32–34 (Feb. 1968).

Selected List
of Useful
Materials

Books and Pamphlets

AHIL (Association of Hospital and Institution Libraries). Hospital Library Standards Committee. *Standards for Library Services in Health Care Institutions.* Chicago: American Library Assn., 1969.
————. Special Committee on Book Selection Criteria. *Materials Selection for Hospital and Institution Libraries.* Chicago: American Library Assn., 1967.
————. Special Committee on Reading Aids for the Handicapped. *Reading Aids for the Handicapped.* 5th rev. ed. Chicago: American Library Assn., 1968.
Abraham, Willard. *The Mentally Retarded Child and Educational Films.* Chicago: Coronet Films, 1966.
Eakin, Mary K. *Good Books for Children.* 3d ed. Chicago: Univ. of Chicago Press, 1966.
Erickson, Marion M., comp. *Annotated Bibliography on Alcoholism and Drug Addiction, June 1969.* Willmar State Hospital: Willmar, Minn. 56201.
Fader, Daniel N., and McNeil, E. B. *Hooked on Books: Program and Proof.* New York: Berkley, 1968.
Goldberg, I. Ignacy. *Selected Bibliography of Special Education.* New York: Columbia Univ. Teachers College Press, 1967.
Goldstein, Herbert, dir. and comp. *The Illinois Plan for Special Education of Exceptional Children: A Curriculum Guide for Teachers of the Educable Mentally Handicapped.* Danville, Ill.: Interstate Printers and Publishers, Inc., n.d.
Kiell, Norman. *The Adolescent through Fiction: A Psychological Approach.* New York: International Universities Press, 1959.
Kircher, Clara J., comp. *Behavior Patterns in Children's Books: A Bibliography.* Washington, D.C.: Catholic Univ. of America Press, 1966.
Leedy, Jack J., ed. *Poetry Therapy: The Use of Poetry in the Treatment of Emotional Disorders.* Philadelphia: Lippincott, 1969.
Library Association. *Hospital Libraries: Recommended Standards for Libraries in Hospitals.* London, Eng.: The Association, 1965.
Luchins, Abraham S. *Group Therapy.* New York: Random, 1964.
Manual of Correctional Standards. 3d ed. Washington, D.C.: American Correctional Association, 1966.

Porterfield, Austin L. *Mirror for Adjustment.* Fort Worth, Tex.: Texas Christian Univ., 1967.

Public Library of Cincinnati and Hamilton County. *Books for Deaf and Hard-of-Hearing Children.* Cincinnati: The Library, 1969.

―――. *Books for Mentally Retarded Children.* Cincinnati: The Library, 1969.

―――. *Books Used for Discussion with Socially Maladjusted Boys, Ages 12–15.* Cincinnati: The Library, n.d.

―――. *Books Used for Discussion with Socially Maladjusted Girls, Ages 12–15.* Cincinnati: The Library, n.d.

Robinson, Helen M., comp. *Developing Permanent Interest in Reading.* Chicago: Univ. of Chicago Press, 1956.

Shrodes, Caroline, ed. *Psychology through Literature.* New York: Oxford Univ. Press, 1943.

Social, Educational Research and Development, Inc. *Institutional Library Services: A Plan for the State of Illinois.* Chicago: American Library Assn., 1970.

Standards for Library-Media Centers in Schools for the Deaf: A Handbook for the Development of Library-Media Programs. Sponsored by the American Instructors of the Deaf. Washington, D.C.: HEW, Office of Education, [1967].

Stefferud, Alfred, ed. *Wonderful World of Books.* New York: New American Library, 1952.

Stone, A. A. and Stone, A. S., eds. *The Abnormal Personality through Literature.* Englewood Cliffs, N.J.: Prentice-Hall, 1966.

United Hospital Fund of New York. *Essentials for Patients' Libraries: A Guide.* New York: The Fund, 1966.

Wettingfeld, Joan. *Library Program for Retarded Children: A Bibliography.* Dansville, N.Y.: Instructor Publications, 1970.

Zaccaria, J. S. and Moses, H. A. *Facilitating Human Development through Reading: The Use of Bibliotherapy in Teaching and Counseling.* Champaign, Ill.: Stipes, 1968.

Periodicals

AHIL Quarterly. American Library Association, 50 East Huron Street, Chicago, Ill. 60611 (with membership only).

American Journal of Correction. American Correctional Association, 1000 Shoreham Bldg., 15th and 8th Streets N.W., Washington, D.C. $5.

American Libraries. American Library Association, 50 East Huron Street, Chicago, Ill. 60611 (with membership only).

Exceptional Children. Council for Exceptional Children, Jefferson Plaza, 1201 16th Street, N.W., Washington, D.C. 20036.

Mental Retardation. American Association on Mental Deficiency, 5201 Connecticut Avenue N.W., Washington, D.C. 20015. $7.

The Pointer. Association for Special Class Teachers and Parents of the Handicapped, Inc., P.O. Box 131, University Station, Syracuse, N.Y. 13210.

Rehabilitation Literature. National Society for Crippled Children and Adults, Inc. 2023 West Ogden Avenue, Chicago, Ill. 60612. $4.50.

Sight-Saving Review. National Society for the Prevention of Blindness, Inc. 16 East 40th Street, New York, N.Y. 10016. $3.50.

Training School Bulletin. American Institute for Mental Studies, Training School Unit, Vineland, N.J. 08360. $3.

Volta Review. Alexander Graham Bell Association for the Deaf, 1537 35th Street N.W., Washington, D.C. 20007. $8.

*Books for
the Troubled Child
and
Adolescent*

Prepared by the SUBCOMMITTEE ON THE TROUBLED CHILD
    Barbara Ambler
    Marilee Foglesong
    Margaret M. Kimmel
    Clara J. Kircher
    Jane Manthorne
    Doris Stotz
    Hilda K. Limper, Chairman

Introduction

Books Subtly Teach as They Entertain

"Truly of all masters books alone are free and freely teach." These words are as applicable today as when they appeared in *Philobiblon,* the work of the fourteenth-century English bishop, Richard de Bury. He speaks in this work of books as masters who "instruct us without whip or rod, without harsh words of anger, asking naught in return." To books he also ascribes other qualities when he says: "If you go astray, they do not chide; if you betray ignorance to them, they know not how to laugh in scorn."

Books have changed greatly since the fourteenth century, and theories about what they can mean to children have been refined. Yet today's workers with children and young people find it still true that books one reads for entertainment or recreation both affect and motivate the reader. Books subtly teach, and not only when read by the child individually. They can also be used to augment the group discussion of problems between young people and those who guide them. Adults working with children and young people are often at a loss to find a common ground for communication. A book with relevant subject matter known to both child and adult can be the means of bridging the gap between generations.

In distinction from their value in imparting information, books have for centuries been used to foster desired attitudes in children. The didactic children's literature of the past has now largely given way to imaginative literature in which, for the perceptive reader, the moral integrity of the characters shines through the details of the plot. In evaluating the therapeutic aspects of reading, Evalene Jackson says: "While didactic literature may have therapeutic effects, imaginative literature makes possible an emotional experience without which therapy cannot take place."[1]

Modern literature for children and young people abounds in situations and problems they are likely to encounter in today's world. The best of this literature is not only good recreational reading, but also serves to help the reader understand himself and the world in which he lives. Through the actions of the characters the reader will often gain some insight into why he behaves as he does. Where this insight also motivates altered and improved attitudes or behavior, the reading of the book results in problem solving and life enrichment, and may be said to be therapeutic.

This process is helped when an adviser or therapist can discuss the book with the reader and lead him to talk about his own problems in terms of the book's characters and situations. If the reader comes to see possible solutions, and lives them out vicariously by envisioning himself in the role of the book's protagonist, he is on the road to finding solutions to his own problems. As Antonia Wenkart has said: "A child can become what he envisions himself to be. Image helps to transform desire into reality."[2] Books alone cannot accomplish this, but can be a strong contributing factor when a warm relationship, as with an adult adviser or trusted friend, is also present.

The Handicapped Child

Book heroes and heroines who have overcome difficulties often serve as inspiration to the handicapped. A child may have come to feel that his particular handicap precludes achievement and a satisfying life. He then may take heart and find new hope in reading a biography of a man like Franklin D. Roosevelt, who, in spite of having been told by his doctor that he would be a helpless invalid following polio, in later years became governor of New York and then president of the United States. Statements in Gerald Johnson's biography of Roosevelt, in which the author writes of Roosevelt's illness and subsequent public career, could well challenge the reader to achievements of his own despite handicaps, or perhaps because of them. Johnson writes:

> In sports, in business, in politics, in war, in peace, in anything, the champion is the fighter who can be beaten to a pulp, cut up, bloodied, and finally knocked flat, but who can get up and fight again.[3]

> . . . One who can whip pain and death will take on anything else and laugh about it; and others, looking on, will begin to suspect that he is unbeatable. Up to this time Roosevelt, as a politician, had not been bad, maybe even a bit of a star. But it was while he was flat on his back in a hospital bed that he became a champion.[4]

Books Break Walls

Again, books can be a source of vicarious experience to a child confined to a hospital or to his home for long periods of time due to illness.

Books can make up for the lack of personal contacts, and a child can vicariously gain much through books which will widen his horizons and augment his life experiences.

Marguerite De Angeli expresses this well in *The Door in the Wall.* In one place a kindly monk, mentor to a young crippled boy, says to him: "Whether thou'lt walk soon I know not. This I know. We must teach thy hands to be skillful in many ways, and we must teach thy mind to go about whether thy legs will carry thee or no. For reading is another door in the wall, dost understand, my son?"[5]

In an article entitled, "Another Door in the Wall,"[6] Josephine Kerr tells how her polio-stricken son found the "door in the wall" of his physical confinement by reading all manner of books. As he mentally traveled far and wide, he broke the "walls" of his confinement again and again until he could relate favorably to almost any situation. This might compare with "preventive medicine" in that reading forestalled the emotional conflict that can come from being ill equipped to meet new situations.

Growing Up and Living with Others

Among the problems peculiar to children which books can help to alleviate are those of growing up and preparing for life as an adult, and the development of healthy relationships with siblings and peers. A child who seeks his fun at the expense of others might see himself in a new light after reading books such as *D.J.'s Worst Enemy,* by Robert Burch, or *Otis Spofford,* by Beverly Cleary, in which the protagonists get their comeuppances. The value of the friendship of one's peers as a solution to the problem of loneliness is suggested in such books as *Jennifer, Hecate, Macbeth, William McKinley, and Me, Elizabeth,* by E. L. Konigsburg and *Noonday Friends,* by Mary Stolz. The assuming of responsibility as a mark of growing maturity is another problem that faces many children. Annie Jenner in *My Brother Stevie,* by Eleanor Clymer, is a character whose acquaintanceship could inspire the reader to put forth effort in this direction.

The Broken Home

In the modern world where divorce and remarriage of parents is a common experience, children must often face the reality of divorce and adjustment to stepparents. Reading about others in similar circumstances can sometimes be helpful by suggesting aspects of their situations of which readers before had no understanding. In Betty Cavanna's *Breath of Fresh Air* the heroine finally accepts her parents' divorce when she comes to realize that they are incompatible. Such a book could be meaningful to a girl in whose family a similar problem exists.

Books can also help the child come to terms with the problem of the acceptance of stepparents by letting him experience vicariously, through reading, mutual love and concern between fictional stepparents and their children. Titles like *Smoke,* by William Corbin, and *Fifer for the Union,* by Lorenzo Allen, can serve admirably in this way.

Children's behavior is often influenced by the problems of their parents, as seen in *Queenie Peavy,* by Robert Burch, and *To Shake a Shadow,* by Phyllis Naylor. The reading of these books can give insight into the reactions of children to parents who are in trouble with the law, and may lead the reader to understand himself better and motivate him toward more responsible behavior should his problems be similar.

The Hostile Child

In situations where there are problems in parent-child relationships, the child often becomes hostile and rebellious. For this reason the bibliography which follows groups together books dealing with the hostile child and those which cover parent-child relationships.

With the hostile, aggressive child in mind, we have included books under the heading "Nature Books for Release of Tension." Experience in working with juvenile delinquents shows that they readily read books in which violence and aggression in nature are described; *Old Yeller,* by Fred Gipson, and *Wild Boy,* by Thomas Fall, are examples. They also like books such as *Avalanche!,* by A. Rutgers van der Loeff, in which young people meet and accept the challenge presented by a natural disaster. This seems to indicate that delinquents derive from such reading some release from their own drives toward violence and aggression. These same books are also helpful when used with crippled children who feel rebellious and angry because of their handicaps. It is sometimes too painful for them to read of others who have similar handicaps, but the reading of books about aggression and violence in nature seems to give them some release from their own feelings. An experience with a paraplegic girl who would read nothing but wild animal stories is but one of several cases that could be cited to bear out this theory.

Preparation for Adulthood

Preparation for life as an adult in today's world must include formal education. Young people who are potential or actual educational dropouts can be made aware of the value of a good education by reading and participating in a discussion of such books as *Runaway Teen,* by Ann Finlayson, or *Drop-out,* by Jeanette Eyerly. These two books concern disenchanted dropouts who decide to return to school because they find out that without a high school education, satisfying and productive employment is out of their reach.

Information on sex and on the responsibilities that come with growing up are also a necessary part of preparation for adulthood. Thus the list contains books which give specific information on sex and growth into manhood and womanhood, as well as fiction dealing with problems created by illicit sexual relationships.

Self-discovery and the feeling of self-worth are other phases of growing up. Understanding others is important, but as Josette Frank says: ". . . to understand others, we must, of course, understand ourselves, and books may be our richest source for self-discovery. All great fiction, perhaps, may be said to hold up a mirror to its readers. But for boys and girls certain books reflect back an image they recognize as themselves."[7] *The Year of the Raccoon,* by Lee Kingman, illustrates how a boy who thinks he has no talents discovers that he has one of life's most important attributes—a strong sense of responsibility. Books containing revelations of this kind could well lead the reader to self-examination and self-discovery.

Choices of Behavior

Young people in slum areas of large cities may feel that the only road open to them is that of joining a gang and living on the streets. Rufus Henry in *Durango Street,* by Frank Bonham, feels this way when on parole from Pine Valley Honor Camp. Readers of his story may glimpse a nonviolent way out, not only for Rufus but also for themselves. Similarly, other books on the list suggest additional healthy outlets as substitutes for violence and delinquency.

Coming to see possible choices of behavior is important. This was well stated by Dr. William Glasser, eminent psychiatrist and author of *Reality Therapy,* in an address given to librarians working with hospital patients and institutional inmates. The mentally ill and those in prison have made bad choices and selected unhealthy avenues of activity because they think no other choices are available, he said. Books open up new worlds, broaden horizons, and increase the scope of choices for behavior. Sell, read, and talk about books, Dr. Glasser urged in speaking of the librarian's relationship with the delinquent. "In discussing books, we are using one of the most basic forms of communication. Be warm and interested in people, work with them, consider your relationship with them and what they are doing. The behavior of reading a book is responsible behavior. Select and push books, and discuss them with the patient. This is the librarian's job."[8]

Group Discussion

If individual counseling sessions are not practical, group discussions centered around books can be an effective means of airing and sharing views and feelings. This is especially true when members of a group have some of the same problems, as with delinquents. It is necessary, of course, to have enough copies of the book so that everyone in the group will have a chance to read it. A small group naturally allows for more participation from each member. The leader must be thoroughly familiar with the selection to keep the discussion going. He will want to ferret out ideas and values from the story, and so direct the questions that these values will be brought out in the discussion. In *Hot Rod,* by Henry Felsen, for example, such values as respect for authority, a sense of responsibility, and good use of a second chance can be discussed in connection with the story. To keep the discussion going, the leader will want to use open-end questions rather than those that may be answered with "yes" or "no." The discussant will thus have a better chance to express himself fully, and his reply may stimulate another person to further expression of an idea. Such discussions are bound to stimulate thought, and may lead to self-examination and to motivation toward a more acceptable and advantageous form of behavior.

The purpose of the following lists, then, is to help teachers, social workers, psychologists and psychiatrists, probation officers, librarians, and others working with children and young people, who wish to use books as part of their counseling technique. The book annotations are designed to provide adequate background for the adult selecting the books. His knowledge of the individual child, coupled with this information, will determine which titles are appropriate. The list is a selective one and consists of titles found effective in work with young people. The books are arranged alphabetically by the name of the author under the respective headings.

Notes

1. Evalene P. Jackson, "Bibliotherapy and Reading Guidance," *Library Trends* 11, no.2: 121 (Oct. 1962).

2. Antonia Wenkart, "The Child Meets the World," in Moustakas, Clark, ed., *Existential Child Therapy* (New York: Basic Books, 1966), p.197.

3. Gerald W. Johnson, *Franklin D. Roosevelt: Portrait of a Great Man* (New York: Morrow, 1967), p.91.

4. Ibid., p.95.

5. Marguerite de Angeli, *The Door in the Wall* (Garden City, N.Y.: Doubleday, 1949), p.29.

6. Josephine S. Kerr, "Another Door in the Wall," *Horn Book* 35, no.6: 497–507 (Dec. 1959).

7. Josette Frank, "Literature of Human Understanding," *Top of the News* (Dec. 1958), p.8.

8. William Glasser, "Reality Therapy as Applied to Hospitalized Patients," *AHIL Quarterly* 8, no.1:9, (Fall 1967).

Adjusting
to Physical
Handicaps

In the case of physically ill patients, a sort of psychological emergency also exists; but these people are not visited by psychiatrists, their psychological needs for readjustment are more or less normal and due to external circumstances; therefore, they do not have the benefit of the expert help of the psychiatrist. The librarian gives them actual psychological treatment through books.

DR. LORE HIRSCH

The Runner, by Jane Annixter. New York: Holiday, 1956. 220p.

> THEME: Boy overcomes effects of polio
> AUDIENCE: Boys and girls
> READING LEVEL: Grades 5–6   INTEREST LEVEL: Ages 10–13

Fourteen-year-old Clem Mayfield is able to overcome almost all the crippling effects of polio, with only a slight lameness in one leg left. In spite of this Clem pulls his share of the work involved in training polo ponies at his uncle's ranch in Wyoming. He is drawn through his love of horses to attempt to tame and train a wild roan colt which he calls "the runner." Throughout his many adventures, trials, and hardships, including a two-day fight to save the horse from a swamp and a grizzly, he refuses to allow his handicap to be an excuse for doing less than the best possible job.

Clem's struggle against his handicap does not come easily, but he refuses to make excuses for himself. His ultimate triumph could be a source of inspiration for other boys who think their handicaps too much for them to handle. The account of the survival of "the runner" and a dog through a Wyoming winter adds excitement to this story of courage.

The Trembling Years, by Elsie Barber. New York: Macmillan, 1949. 237p.

> THEME: College girl learns to live with handicap
> AUDIENCE: Girls
> READING LEVEL: Grade 7   INTEREST LEVEL: Ages 12 up

Kathy Storm, seventeen and a freshman in college, is stricken with polio during the excitement of the first days of the school year. Paralysis sets in and Kathy feels her world has collapsed. People stare at her in her wheel chair, and even her boy friend makes excuses not to come and see her. Bitterly rebelling against her handicap, she gives way to self-pity. Finally she realizes that, no matter how helpful people are, in the end she has to rely on herself. Then she summons her will power, determines to walk alone, goes back to college, and wins a real victory.

Girls who are discouraged and are struggling to live with problems will identify with Kathy. This is a story of romance, as well as of courage.

Reach for the Sky, by Paul Brickhill. New York: Norton, 1954. 312p.
> THEME: A man's achievements in spite of loss of both legs
> AUDIENCE: Boys
> READING LEVEL: Grade 8   INTEREST LEVEL: Ages 13 up

Douglas Bader is an extraordinary young man who plays golf, swims, drives a car, dances, and flies an airplane. These accomplishments are not startling, except for the fact that Douglas lost both legs in a plane crash in 1931. Determined to do everything he did before the accident, Douglas showed remarkable inventiveness in achieving his goal. During World War II he was twice taken prisoner, only to escape twice. Finally recaptured, he spent the duration of the war in Colditz.

An almost unbelievable story, all the more inspiring because it is true.

Silent Storm, by Marion M. Brown. New York: Abingdon, 1963. 250p.
> THEME: Two women face handicaps of deafness and blindness
> AUDIENCE: Girls and some boys
> READING LEVEL: Grades 5–6   INTEREST LEVEL: Ages 11 up

Anne Sullivan, Helen Keller's famous teacher, came from humble beginnings, having spent part of her early years in an almshouse, with no formal education until she was twelve. Further handicapped by poor sight which required repeated surgery, Miss Sullivan was nevertheless graduated from Perkins Institute as valedictorian of her class. With little special preparation, she then undertook the gargantuan job of teaching deaf-blind Helen Keller. With patience, a spirit of determination, and resourcefulness she reached her highly intelligent pupil, and led her to graduation from Radcliffe College and a writing career.

Anne Sullivan Macy has been called "the miracle worker," and this compelling biography shows her achieving the near impossible task of penetrating Helen Keller's wall of silence and darkness, despite her own afflictions. It should inspire many a handicapped youth.

Note: Another good book about Anne Sullivan Macy and Helen Keller is: *Valiant Companions,* by Helen E. Waite. Philadelphia: Macrae Smith, 1959. 223p.

The Secret Garden, by Frances H. Burnett. Philadelphia: Lippincott, 1911 and 1962. 256p.

> THEME: Two lonely, unhappy children find health and happiness through interest in one another and in the out-of-doors
>
> AUDIENCE: Girls and boys

READING LEVEL: Grade 5   INTEREST LEVEL: Ages 9–12

An unloved and unloving orphan, Mary Lennox, comes to live in the unhappy home of an uncle on the English moors. Here she finds a long-deserted secret garden where she develops an interest in growing things and discovers the satisfactions of liking someone, new experiences for her. She befriends a peasant boy who loves all creatures of the woods and fields. Together the two bring Mary's invalid cousin to the secret garden, where fresh air, sunshine, and new interests work "magic" for both cousins.

The story still has considerable appeal and a message for its readers, especially lonely, self-centered children.

Sink it, Rusty, by Matt Christopher. Boston: Little, 1963. 138p.

> THEME: Boy overcomes crippling effects of polio
>
> AUDIENCE: Boys

READING LEVEL: Grades 3–4   INTEREST LEVEL: Ages 8–11

Rusty Young, although only slightly crippled by polio, magnifies his inadequacies when he tries to compete with his friends on a basketball court. Anxious to participate in the games, he feels he is not wanted and is easily hurt. Through the careful and judicious help of Alex Daws, whose own basketball career was cut short by the loss of his left hand, Rusty is encouraged to make use of the capabilities he has and proves himself a strong team member, becoming the hero of the final game.

No miracle cure or pat solutions are offered. The realistic advice to do what one can do without becoming discouraged is valuable for boys whose handicaps prevent them from leading lives as active as those of their peers. The change in Rusty's attitudes toward his handicap as a result of his emphasis on his accomplishments will provide encouragement.

Finding My Way: An Autobiography, by Borghild Dahl. New York: Dutton, 1962. 121p.

> THEME: A woman, suddenly blind, makes a good life for herself
>
> AUDIENCE: Girls

READING LEVEL: Grades 5–7   INTEREST LEVEL: Ages 12–15

A moving and inspiring story of how the author made a life for herself after becoming blind. At her insistence she maintains her own apartment, lives her own life, learns how to cook and iron, and even takes trips by herself. At each step she is tempted to give up and ask for help, but she makes herself take on the responsibility of her own care, and finds new pride in her abilities. The last chapter contains practical suggestions for blind people on how to plan their lives and on ways to improve their attitude toward their handicap.

This story of a courageous woman who overcame her handicaps could be a source of inspiration and hope to others who seem doomed to a sideline life.

Door in the Wall, by Marguerite de Angeli. New York: Doubleday, 1949.
THEME: Crippled son of an English nobleman wins knighthood through courage
AUDIENCE: Boys and girls
READING LEVEL: Grades 4–5   INTEREST LEVEL: Ages 9–12

Set in thirteenth-century England, this is the story of young Robin, who is crippled by an illness while his parents are away serving their king. Robin's care is taken over by Brother Luke, a perceptive monk who teaches him craftsmanship and reading, saying: "We must teach thy hands to be skillful in many ways, and must teach thy mind to go about whether thy legs will carry thee or no. For reading is another door in the wall. . . ." Robin learns, gains the bravery to carry out a very courageous act which saves his people from an enemy, and earns knighthood for himself. Thus Robin finds the "door in the wall" of his physical disability.

An inspiring story of courage and victory over a physical handicap. Beautiful illustrations help make the text come alive.

Seeing Fingers: The Story of Louis Braille, by Etta DeGering. New York: McKay, 1962. 115p.
THEME: Blind Louis Braille works out a successful system of finger reading
AUDIENCE: Boys and girls
READING LEVEL: Grade 5   INTEREST LEVEL: Ages 10 up

Born in France in 1809, the son of a village harness maker, Louis Braille was accidentally blinded between the ages of three and four in his father's shop. An alert child, he learned fast in spite of his handicap, and loved stories. When he started to school he was disappointed that there were no books that he could read himself. Later, at the Royal Institute for the Blind, he found only a few bulky books with raised letters. Eager to have many books which he and his classmates could read, Braille, while only sixteen, worked out an embossed alphabet based on different arrangements of six raised dots which could be reproduced on heavy paper. At twenty he had perfected a system for writing words and music for the blind which eventually became standard all over the world.

Louis Braille's life illustrates what motivation can contribute to inventiveness, and is dramatic proof that a physical handicap does not preclude high achievement.

Johnny Tremain, by Esther Forbes. Boston: Houghton, 1943. 256p.

      THEME: A boy endures injury and sudden alienation from friends

    AUDIENCE: Boys and girls

READING LEVEL: Grade 6   INTEREST LEVEL: Ages 12 up

The boy flings himself down next to his mother's unmarked grave and weeps. He weeps because of his loneliness and his recent reversal of fortune. He weeps over the burned, maimed hand which seems to spell the end of his future. The boy is Johnny Tremain, recently a skilled, arrogant apprentice in the silversmith trade. The time is 1773 in Boston, when a surge toward independence will soon turn young and old, sturdy folk and cripples, into patriots.

This notable historical novel follows Johnny's story and the birth pangs of the new nation. The desolation faced by the fourteen-year-old lad is real, and his conquest of self-pity invites emulation. Boys will understand the overwhelming scope of one boy's courage when Johnny joins brave men in revolution and at last readies himself for surgery.

Kristy's Courage, by Babbis Friis. New York: Harcourt, 1965. 159p.

      THEME: Badly disfigured girl faces and overcomes the teasing of others

    AUDIENCE: Girls

READING LEVEL: Grades 5–6   INTEREST LEVEL: Ages 10–12

Struck by a car, seven-year-old Kristy Momark has to start second grade with a deep scar on one cheek and a tongue so swollen she cannot talk intelligibly. Not realizing what she looks like to others and how badly her speech is impeded, Kristy is confused and hurt when she hears other children laugh at her. Cruel teasing by older boys and her mother's absence in the hospital with a new baby combine to make life unbearable for Kristy, so she returns to the hospital and the friend who was so good to her. In the hospital the surgeon gives her a fake bandage which will elicit sympathy instead of taunts. After wearing it for a couple of days, Kristy realizes that the bandage is a cheat and voluntarily takes it off. The children have become used to her appearance by now, and with a clear conscience she fits back easily into school life.

Kristy's bewilderment at the treatment she receives and her courageous decision to see it through without subterfuge provide a basis for discussion on how people react to handicaps in other people, and also provide inspiration for those whose appearance has caused them to keep apart from others.

Follow My Leader, by James B. Garfield. New York: Viking, 1957. 191p.
    THEME: Blind boy's adjustment to his handicap
    AUDIENCE: Boys
READING LEVEL: Grades 5–6   INTEREST LEVEL: Ages 10–13

Blinded by an exploding firecracker, Jimmy Carter rebelliously rejects attempts to help him adjust to his new condition. Always a leader in school and sports, he cannot see how he will be able to live an active life again. The first break in his hostility is prompted by the information that he can have a guide dog. From then on, all his energies are directed to proving himself worthy of one; learning to walk with a cane, learning Braille, and doing chores around the house. With each accomplishment his sense of self-confidence grows and he is able to joke about his handicap.

At the guide-dog school the dog, Leader, is given to him, and Jimmy's happiness grows and he works hard to learn how to become one unit with the dog. At the same time, he is able to forgive the boy who threw the firecracker and so conquers an internal handicap.

Jimmy's slow but steady adjustment and return to near-normal life could provide inspiration for other blind children. His example of accomplishment will be a source of help for all readers with handicaps to use what they have to the fullest.

King of the Wind, by Marguerite Henry. Chicago: Rand McNally, 1948. 173p.
    THEME: A small mute stable boy is responsible for noteworthy accomplishment
    AUDIENCE: Boys and girls
READING LEVEL: Grades 5–6   INTEREST LEVEL: Ages 10–14

From the time of his birth in the stables of the Sultan of Morocco, Sham, a spirited red-gold stallion, was cared for with great affection by Agba, a little mute stable boy. Because of a white spot on Sham's heel Agba predicted that he would be as "swift as the wind"; but the foal also had "the wheat ear" on his chest, and superstition held that this was an omen of evil. Both markings seemed fateful to Sham's future, for much evil did, indeed, come to him as he went from one master to another until he sired a colt that became a winner at the English Newmarket races. Then, as the famous Godolphin Arabian, he was the ancestor to such racing winners as Man o' War, and became truly the "King of the Wind."

Even though mute, Agba made himself understood, and because of his great love for Sham and efforts on his behalf, the Arabian's name stands high in the history of famous race horses.

The Man Who Fought Back: Red Schoendienst, by Al Hirshberg. New York: Messner, 1961. 192p.

    THEME: Noted baseball player conquers illness

    AUDIENCE: Boys

READING LEVEL: Grade 7   INTEREST LEVEL: Ages 12–17

A red-haired, freckle-faced farm boy, Red Schoendienst spent his boyhood fishing in the Kaskaskia River in Germantown, Illinois, and playing baseball. Called a "boy straight out of the pages of Mark Twain," he preferred sports to learning. His baseball career started when he was in his teens and rapidly took him to the front ranks of the St. Louis Cardinals and the Milwaukee Braves as one of the great second basemen. What distinguished him as a player and as a man was Red's fierce resistance to handicap. Repeatedly he was injured and repeatedly he regained his health. In his bravest battle against illness he defeated tuberculosis, and after a year as an invalid he returned to the game.

This life story is put together with the authenticity of ball games and pennant races, with the animation of colorful personalities such as Stan Musial and Frank Lane, and the brisk on-the-scene dialogue.

The Child of the Silent Night, by Edith Fisher Hunter. Boston: Houghton, 1963. 124p.

    THEME: How learning comes to blind-deaf-mute child

    AUDIENCE: Boys and girls

READING LEVEL: Grade 4   INTEREST LEVEL: Ages 8–10

Laura Bridgman was like a child in a room without windows or doors, for she could neither see, hear, nor speak. Uncle Asa, a neighbor, was convinced she could learn, however, and set out to teach her as best he could. James Barrett, a student at a nearby college, became interested in Laura and brought her to Dr. Samuel Gridley Howe at the Perkins Institute for the Blind. Here it was that Laura learned that objects have names and that one mind can communicate with another. Nearly forty years later another blind and deaf child named Helen Keller had a door opened for her because there was positive proof that such a child could learn.

Laura's story is told with warmth and admiration for the inspired teaching and the intelligent little girl who benefited from it.

Karen, by Marie Killilea. New York: Prentice-Hall, 1952. 314p.

    THEME: Cerebral palsied child learns to adjust to handicap

    AUDIENCE: Girls

READING LEVEL: Grade 6   INTEREST LEVEL: Ages 10 up

Karen, second child of Marie and Jimmy Killilea, is born with cerebral palsy. Confident that something can be done to help, the couple go from one specialist to another. Some tell them to forget they ever had a child; others offer quack remedies; none are encouraging. Then Doctor B. enters their lives and gives them the hope and encouragement they need. Through his efforts and the hard work of the Killileas, Karen responds to treatment. Obstacle after obstacle is overcome. Karen's moment of triumph comes when she announces: "I can walk, I can talk, I can read, I can write. I can do anything."

Despite her handicap and the necessary extra attention she must receive, Karen manages to grow up without being selfish or filled with self-pity. Understandably her family and friends delight in her progress. Karen is a special child, and hers is an extraordinary story.

With Love from Karen is a sequel to *Karen.*

The Shining Moment, by Mildred Lawrence. New York: Harcourt, 1960. 187p.

THEME: A girl copes with a scarred face and a scarred personality
AUDIENCE: Girls
READING LEVEL: Grade 6   INTEREST LEVEL: Ages 12–17

"I could see my life stretching ahead of me, bright and sunshiny, like summertime going on forever. On that thought I should have knocked on wood again, because it was the last wonderful thought I was going to have for a long time." In the car accident which follows, pretty redhaired Janey Kirsten sees her hopes of winning beauty contests dashed to pieces, her cheek marred with an ugly, livid cut. Instead of returning to Florida and the university, Janey stays with her grandmother in North Carolina to hide. A job with the local newspaper leads her to wholehearted involvement in establishing a community college and in gem-hunting with a local young man.

As her year of hiding progresses, Janey finds that her scar is fading, and she supplants her old skin-deep values with new respect for work, intellect, and friendship.

Corn-Farm Boy, by Lois Lenski. Philadelphia: Lippincott, 1954. 180p.

THEME: A rheumatic fever victim learns to accept and realistically
          adjust to his physical difficulty
AUDIENCE: Boys and girls
READING LEVEL: Grades 4–5   INTEREST LEVEL: Ages 9–12

Dick Hoffman lives on an Iowa corn farm where he enjoys driving a tractor. In addition, he cares for the animals, and always has several pets. With him constantly is the threat of an attack of rheumatic fever, which sometimes disables him or puts him on crutches for weeks at a time. After an accident caused by his chest pains and momentary blackout, Dick realizes that he does not have the physical stamina for farming, which requires the operation of powerful machines. He will, instead, follow his bent to care for animals and become a veterinarian.

The hard work and everyday adventures of farm life are interwoven with Dick's struggle against physical weakness. An understanding mother helps him to face and adjust to his problem. Readers may capture his courage in making a difficult decision.

Mine for Keeps, by Jean Little. Boston: Little, 1962. 186p.

THEME: A cerebral palsy victim conquers her fears of new situations

AUDIENCE: Girls

READING LEVEL: Grades 4–5   INTEREST LEVEL: Ages 9–11

"Scary Sarey" is what she has been called, and Sarah Jane Copeland is afraid the title still fits her. Coming home after five years in a special school would create problems even if one didn't have to cope with braces and crutches required by cerebral palsy. But Sal receives a small dog, Susie, who is even more scared than she, and with the help of new friends, she manages to train Susie and help another child out of his shell. In doing so she helps herself.

Sal's efforts on behalf of others help her overcome her own fears and physical limitations. Her family is especially real and understanding without being too protective.

Golden Mare, by William Corbin McGraw. New York: Coward, 1955. 122p.

THEME: The love between a gentle old horse and a boy with rheumatic fever, bringing achievement to both

AUDIENCE: Boys and girls

READING LEVEL: Grade 5   INTEREST LEVEL: Ages 10–13

Robin, a victim of rheumatic fever, must limit his activities and cannot ride a horse at great speed as do his brothers, so aging Magic, the golden mare, is a perfect mount for him. Great affection and understanding develop between the two, and Robin gains some emotional security from his relationship with the horse. In a time of crisis, it is Magic who helps Robin achieve the near-impossible feat of bringing help to his injured mother during a severe snowstorm. Through this incident Robin earns new respect and affection from his hitherto indifferent brothers. They in turn help him to face Magic's death.

A story to illustrate the powers of love between a boy and an animal, and the possibilities of brave achievement for one with physical limitations.

Electrical Genius of Liberty Hall: Charles Proteus Steinmetz, by Floyd Miller. New York: McGraw-Hill, 1962. 126p.

> THEME: A crippled man of slight physical stature realizes unprecedented achievement in his chosen field
>
> AUDIENCE: Boys and girls
>
> READING LEVEL: Grade 6   INTEREST LEVEL: Ages 11 up

Born a hunchback in Bismarck's Germany, Charles Steinmetz remained small and physically crippled throughout his lifetime. Mentally he was a genius, and early showed a great gift for mathematics. After he came to America as a political refugee, his gifts were soon discovered and he was given a chance to contribute to the growing knowledge of electrical engineering. His calculations and experiments on alternating current provided the knowledge necessary to send current over great distances, and made possible the widespread use of electricity today.

Steinmetz's deformity was hereditary, so he preferred not to marry. He adopted a son, however, and as a father and grandfather became an important part of a family to whom he gave great love. He was honored at his death for his scientific achievements, his patience, and his generosity. His biographer writes: "Steinmetz's entire life had been an avowal of love, and he was loved in return. No man can earn a greater epitaph."

The Helen Keller Story, by Catherine Owens Peare. New York: Crowell, 1959. 183p.

> THEME: The amazing life of deaf-blind Helen Keller
>
> AUDIENCE: Girls
>
> READING LEVEL: Grades 5–6   INTEREST LEVEL: Ages 10–13

Switching from Helen's point of view to her teacher's and to that of an objective observer, the author covers the whole life of Helen Keller, deaf and blind from early childhood. The sections on Helen's sense of frustration at being unable to communicate her thoughts and feelings and her eagerness once the world of words and ideas is opened are particularly vivid.

Miss Keller's determination to overcome all obstacles, her refusal to be discouraged, and her success in a world of doubters will provide inspiration not only to blind or deaf children but to all children whose handicaps seem to bring their lives to dead ends. To Helen "impossible" meant "do it," a point made very clear in this readable and moving book.

The FDR Story, by Catherine Owens Peare. New York: Crowell, 1962. 245p.

    THEME: High achievement in the face of physical handicap
    AUDIENCE: Boys and girls
READING LEVEL: Grade 6   INTEREST LEVEL: Ages 11–17

Franklin Roosevelt's life story began like the idyll of a modern prince: wealthy parents, education at Groton and Harvard, marriage to a debutante with the President of the United States in attendance, and a rapid rise in politics. But the idyll ended when a severe attack of polio struck Roosevelt down. He could become an almost immobile country squire, as his mother wished, or he could strengthen his limbs and learn to use crutches and braces, as his wife Eleanor wished. FDR chose the painful, sometimes humiliating route back to active life, and eventually to the Presidency, by making his crippled body take second place to his vigorous mind and spirit.

Although this brief biography covers FDR's whole lifetime, particular emphasis is placed on his conquest of his handicap and on the concern for humanity which his own suffering engendered. "Suddenly, he was one of those who needed to be helped. . . . He was developing a whole new viewpoint on the 'have-nots' of the world."

Note: Another good biography of Franklin Roosevelt is:
Franklin D. Roosevelt: Portrait of a Great Man, by Gerald Johnson. New York: Morrow, 1967. 185p.

David in Silence, by Veronica Robinson. Philadelphia: Lippincott, 1966. 126p.

    THEME: Adjustment of children to a deaf newcomer
    AUDIENCE: Boys and girls
READING LEVEL: Grades 5–6   INTEREST LEVEL: Ages 10–13

Michael is looking forward to having a boy of his own age around when the new neighbors move in. Then he sees the red-headed boy who won't speak, the boy who doesn't even seem to know the other children of the neighborhood are around. "He's deaf and dumb. He makes noises like a pig," taunts Paul, and almost before Michael knows it, he is forced into championing David Williams, the new boy next door. Sometimes the children are embarrassed by David's bursts of wild laughter or unintelligible words. Sometimes, as at a local soccer game, misunderstandings lead to ugliness. "But imagine not being able to hear what *we* don't even listen to— your toes scratching on the sheet at night or the beat of your heart. What *do* you listen to when you're deaf?" asks Michael.

David in Silence speaks eloquently for the child confined to a soundless world. The children learn of David's fears and gain more than a little respect for him. On occasion the story teaches its lesson rather pointedly, but this does not detract from a moving account of a deaf boy's search for acceptance.

The Light, by Jeanne Saint-Marcoux. New York: Vanguard, 1958. 158p.

    THEME: Girl adjusts to blindness aided by the one who caused it

    AUDIENCE: Girls

READING LEVEL: Grade 7   INTEREST LEVEL: Ages 12 up

Smuggling is quite a profitable business in the Basque mountains, and Luis Miguel leads the whole operation. One day, while fleeing from a customs official, he accidentally knocks down Mire, a goat girl, and blinds her. Guilt-ridden when he discovers what he has done, he puts the girl in the care of his mother. Up to this time Luis's life has had no direction, school has held no interest; smuggling has been his only concern. The accident changes his whole outlook, and he decides to become an eye surgeon. Mire, too, reaches outside herself and becomes interested in a deaf and dumb child; she is able to identify with the child's problem and breaks through into her silent world. Though Luis and Mire find happiness in devoting their lives to others, they are jubilant when Luis is able to perform a delicate, experimental operation that restores Mire's sight.

Children with visual problems will share Mire's bewilderment at having light suddenly snatched away. Also, children who have caused casualties to another will identify with Luis' guilt feelings. The courage of both young people to face their problems realistically and overcome them is compellingly shown.

Martin Rides the Moor, by Vian Smith. Garden City, N.Y.: Doubleday, 1965. 181p.

    THEME: Deaf boy loses resentment and shut-in feeling with the help of a pony of his own

    AUDIENCE: Boys and girls

READING LEVEL: Grade 5   INTEREST LEVEL: Ages 10–13

Set on the Devonshire moor, this is the story of Martin, bewildered and embittered when at eleven an accident leaves him deaf. In an effort to help Martin adjust, his father buys him a Dartmoor pony. Unresponsive at first, Martin soon becomes attached to the pony in spite of himself, and learns to ride her over the moor, often with a young horsewoman. The attachment between boy and pony becomes stronger when the latter saves Martin's life in a bog. In turn, Martin saves his pony, and through this comes to know the joy of owning her foal.

As Martin finds a sense of security in his close relationship with his pony, his life takes on a new richness, and he feels less confined by his deafness.

Warrior Scarlet, by Rosemary Sutcliff. New York: Walck, 1958. 207p.

THEME: Bronze Age boy attempts to prove his worth in spite of withered arm

AUDIENCE: Boys and girls

READING LEVEL: Grades 7–8   INTEREST LEVEL: Ages 12–15

Drem knows he will have to pass the wolf test to prove himself worthy of the scarlet cloak worn by the men of the tribe. Then he overhears his grandfather complain that his grandson will never be a warrior because of his withered arm, and begins to have his own doubts. At the test, when each boy must kill a wolf without help from another, Drem's best friend Jertrix steps in to save him from certain death. This intervention means Drem has failed and, according to custom, will become an outcast. In a dramatic climax the boy proves his value to the tribe and is awarded the scarlet cloak.

Bronze Age Britain is the setting for this forceful story of a boy becoming a man. His handicap forces Drem to prove, not only his worth, but the intrinsic value of a human being regardless of physical weakness.

A Long Way Up: The Story of Jill Kinmont, by Evans G. Valens. New York: Harper, 1966. 245p.

THEME: Potential Olympic skier becomes paraplegic

AUDIENCE: Girls and boys

READING LEVEL: Grade 8   INTEREST LEVEL: Ages 12 up

Setting her sights on the 1956 Winter Olympic team seemed a natural ambition for Jill Kinmont. Since her fifteenth year she had been practicing more and more, skiing better and better, and consistently winning meets. Because she was also pretty and friendly, she soon became a favorite and was considered a person to watch. Then suddenly it all ended. Participating in a meet, she began her jump too late, was thrown off balance, and crashed to the ground. Her spinal cord severed, Jill was completely and permanently paralyzed from the shoulders down. From her hospital bed she made her decision to return to school and attempt to rebuild her life. Graduating from UCLA, she began a successful teaching career from an electric wheelchair at the Clinic School of the University. The way up was long and strenuous, but Jill Kinmont was equal to the climb.

The world of the ski meet may be foreign to some, but everyone will find meaning in Jill's courage and determination.

A Rainbow for Robin, by Marguerite Vance. New York: Dutton, 1966. 88p.

THEME: A blind girl's accomplishments

AUDIENCE: Girls

READING LEVEL: Grades 3–4   INTEREST LEVEL: Ages 10–13

Robin, blind from birth, learns to use her abilities to participate to the fullest in the world around her. She swims, crochets, acts in plays, and attends a regular school. Her first and strongest love, however, is her music. At an early age she learns to read music in Braille and from then on not only plays the piano but also composes music. Her major triumph occurs when her composition wins first prize in a contest and is played by the local symphony orchestra. She performs at a recital and, as the culmination of her dreams, is asked to play with the orchestra at a future contest.

Although a trifle sweet at times, Robin's story could provide hope and encouragement to blind children who feel that they are cut off from normal activities. Stressed throughout are good family relationships and positive attitudes toward the blind.

Windows for Rosemary, by Marguerite Vance. New York: Dutton, 1956. 60p.

THEME: Blind girl's adjustment to her handicap

AUDIENCE: Girls

READING LEVEL: Grades 3–4   INTEREST LEVEL: Ages 8–11

Nine-year-old Rosemary, born blind, tells of her life in a warm and loving family and of how she participates fully in the joy of living. Rosemary's fondest wish is for a typewriter, and as her birthday nears she is almost afraid to hope for it. The family celebrates her birthday with a special breakfast and party. The day is made perfect by the gift of a typewriter which sets Rosemary on the way to becoming "a great writer," as she hopes.

The matter-of-fact attitude of Rosemary and her family toward blindness will help other children develop a healthy attitude toward their handicaps, and will give normal children a better understanding of the blind.

Run with the Ring, by Kathryn Vinson. New York: Harcourt, 1965. 255p.

THEME: Bitterness can be as handicapping as blindness

AUDIENCE: Boys

READING LEVEL: Grade 7   INTEREST LEVEL: Ages 12–14

Running track and operating a ham radio are the most important things in Mark Mansfield's life until an accidental fall during a track meet blinds him. Doctors claim muscle fatigue caused the fall, but Mark is sure another member of the team fouled him. Bitter and determined to race again, even if he must use a guide ring, Mark persuades his family to send him to the Bayshore Academy for the Deaf and Blind.

Mark's struggle is not only with physical blindness, but also with a kind of spiritual sightlessness. He will not, or cannot, accept the accident as such, but convinces himself that life has handed him an especially raw deal. For a time his evaluation of those around him is obscured by bitterness, but he comes to terms with his blindness and in the final test is big enough to accept himself as he is and forgive his former enemy.

Dead End Bluff, by Elizabeth Witheridge. New York: Atheneum, 1966. 186p.

      THEME: Blind boy discovers that he can find his way out of most of the "dead ends" his blindness seems to pose

      AUDIENCE: Boys and some girls

READING LEVEL: Grade 5–6   INTEREST LEVEL: Ages 11–15

Teen-age Quig is blind, but has a fierce determination to live as normal a life as possible in spite of it. An excellent swimmer, he overcomes his fear of hitting the raft, competes in the free-style race, and wins a trophy for his home town. In spite of the opposition of an overprotective father, he secures and successful discharges the duties of a summer job caring for a litter of thoroughbred elkhounds. When the puppies are stolen from the kennel, Quigs' keen senses of hearing and smell provide the clues for their recovery. Finally, in an emergency he does the thing he most fears: he goes down Dead End Bluff near his home when it is necessary to rescue his young brother from drowning.

Quig's story and the healthy attitudes of his friends are believable. Readers with any physical handicap may be helped to find openings in the "dead ends" of their lives.

A young person's relations with his own age group become increasingly important as he advances from infancy toward adolescent years. During adolescence a person's dealings with his peers become even more significant.

ARTHUR T. JERSILD

The Loser, by Elizabeth Allen. New York: Dutton, 1965. 128p.

THEME: Conformity to peer standards

AUDIENCE: Girls

READING LEVEL: Grade 6   INTEREST LEVEL: Ages 11–17

When the popular high school beauty queen Deirdre Ames meets Denny Hawks, Harvard dropout, her world abruptly changes. Denny introduces her to folk singers, to art, and to poetry. He makes her aware of people and their potential, of her environment and its falseness. Dazzled by his glib tongue and unique manner and dress, Deirdre is blind to his faults and resents having them pointed out to her. Only when Denny runs away from home are her eyes opened to his lies. Confused and hurt, Deirdre gradually comes to realize that knowing Denny has matured her. He has made her stretch and reach and listen, and she will never forget him.

A perceptive and readable novel with which many teen-agers can identify. In spite of normal clashes, a warm relationship exists between Deirdre and her sister.

Screwball, by Alberta Armer. Cleveland: World, 1963. 202p.

THEME: Handicapped boy's achieving the recognition of his peers

AUDIENCE: Boys

READING LEVEL: Grade 5   INTEREST LEVEL: Ages 10–14

Patrick is the kind of boy who can do almost anything, Mike decides. It's hard enough having him for a brother, but Patrick is his twin, and Mike finds the situation almost too much. When the family leaves the farm for Detroit, Mike feels that he must prove himself all over again. Because polio affected his right side, he's unable to play ball, but he has always been good with his hands and takes up soap-box racing as a hobby. In the Detroit soap-box-derby runoff, Mike competes and wins over Patrick. Even before he wins, Mike discovers that making one's best effort is more important than winning the race.

Mike becomes aware of the fact that he can't compete on the same terms as other boys, and although jealous of his brother's athletic ability, he is sensitive enough to realize that Patrick, too, has many problems and often needs more encouragement than he receives.

Castaway Christmas, by Margaret Baker. New York: Farrar, 1963. 158p.
      THEME: Survival and growth to maturity
    AUDIENCE: Boys and girls
READING LEVEL: Grades 5–6   INTEREST LEVEL: Ages 11–13

Because their parents are away most of the year, teen-age Lincoln and Miranda and their ten-year-old sister Pinks attend boarding school in England and look forward with particular pleasure to their Christmas holidays when the family will be together.

On their arrival home in a heavy downpour, they discover that the countryside is flooded and that there is no word from their parents, who have been detained in France. Faced with a cold house and little food, the three try to keep themselves warm and fed. In their anxiety and discomfort they lash out at one another, but throughout their ordeal, their relationship remains that of three ordinary brothers and sisters. Lincoln is bossy; Miranda is fussy; Pinks is a pest. As the emergency continues, however, each finds that his or her contribution is necessary to the survival of all, and they give one another grudging respect for these efforts. By the time their parents arrive, the three are no longer quarreling but have settled into a working relationship of mutual respect.

An exciting and readable story that portrays the growing realization on the part of all three children that each is an individual with definite contributions to make to the family.

D.J.'s Worst Enemy, by Robert Burch. New York: Viking, 1965. 142p.
      THEME: Boy's coming to understand self and being a part of his
            family
    AUDIENCE: Boys and girls
READING LEVEL: Grade 4   INTEREST LEVEL: Ages 9–12

D.J. Madison and his sidekick Nutty try their best to scare Clare Mae, D.J.'s older sister, with an imitation of the old bull from the lower meadow.

The plan backfires when D.J.'s younger brother, Skinny Little Renfroe, manages to scare *them*. That's how it always is—D.J. getting bested by somebody. Renfroe gets in D.J.'s way once too often, however, and when Renfroe ends up in the hospital, D.J. decides to reform.

Here is a real boy who discovers his worst enemy is not family or friends, but himself. Those who find it a trial to be "part of the family" will see D.J. as a kindred spirit and may find new direction in his decision.

Beezus and Ramona, by Beverly Cleary. New York: Morrow, 1955. 159p.

> THEME: Resentment by older sister of her younger sister's attention-getting activities
> AUDIENCE: Girls, sometimes boys
> READING LEVEL: Grade 4   INTEREST LEVEL: Ages 9–11

Nine-year-old Beatrice Quimby, known as Beezus, finds her four-year-old sister, Ramona, a major problem in her life. Ramona makes herself the center of attention and is constantly praised by other people for her "cute" ways and her imagination. On her tenth birthday, after Ramona has ruined two birthday cakes, Beezus tells her mother and Aunt Beatrice of her problem. This leads the two adults to disclose that when they were children they had similar problems. With the knowledge that she need not always feel love for Ramona, Beezus becomes more relaxed and adopts a new attitude toward her.

Relationships between sisters are rarely smooth, and many girls are faced with similar situations about which they may feel guilty and to which they may react in a hostile manner. Mrs. Quimby's common-sense and practical approach to Beezus' problems might help the readers to resolve their own problems and, as Beezus did, adopt a freer and less compulsive relationship with their sisters. The many humorous episodes in the book make it light reading.

Otis Spofford, by Beverly Cleary. New York: Morrow, 1953. 191p.

> THEME: Boy's getting his "comeuppance" for teasing his peers
> AUDIENCE: Boys and girls
> READING LEVEL: Grades 3–4   INTEREST LEVEL: Ages 8–12

Otis likes to stir up excitement. While his mother is working away from home, Mrs. Brewster, manager of the apartment house, keeps an eye on Otis after school. But Mrs. Brewster doesn't like dirt, dogs, or noise, and so Otis seeks attention at school. There is the time, for instance, that his teacher catches him throwing spitballs and Otis finds himself at the back of the room, ordered to make spitballs all afternoon. And the time he catches Ellen Tebbits and cuts her hair, or when he and Stewy, as the two parts of a bull, change the script at the PTA meeting performance. But everyone says he'll get his comeuppance, and sure enough, that's what happens.

Otis and his friends are normal, mischievous children. Parents and teachers are interested, but generally removed from the action. There is a give and take between the children, and the situations are humorous and light. A good, easy, funny book with a message.

My Brother Stevie, by Eleanor Clymer. New York: Holt, 1967. 76p.

    THEME: Girl's responsibility for younger brother

    AUDIENCE: Girls and boys

READING LEVEL: Grade 4   INTEREST LEVEL: Ages 10–14

"Take care of your brother" is what Annie Jenner's mother made her promise. But Annie finds it isn't easy, especially with a boy like Stevie who fools around with candy machines and throws rocks in subways. It takes sympathetic insight from Miss Stover, Stevie's third-grade teacher, to help Annie to understand him a little better.

This is a simple story told in the straightforward manner and language of a twelve-year-old. Any child who has had responsibility for another will readily recognize Annie and will understand that when she says, "Stevie is still a pain in the neck," she says it with hope for his future and her own.

Stepsister Sally, by Helen Daringer. New York: Harcourt, 1966. 182p.

    THEME: The adjustment of two families to each other

    AUDIENCE: Girls

READING LEVEL: Grade 4   INTEREST LEVEL: Ages 9–11

The thought of a brand-new sister, and one just her own age, makes leaving Gran a little more bearable for Sally. Ever since her mother died, she has been living with her grandmother, but now her father has remarried and Sally is to live with her new family. Dorothy, the oldest girl, isn't as interested as Sally in having or being a stepsister. Her new brother, Don, accepts Sally but is reluctant to give up his position as head of the family. It isn't until the track meet in which Sally's class is competing that an understanding is reached, and Dorothy claims Sally as her "really true sister."

The writing is a bit stilted and old-fashioned at times, but Sally and Dorothy and their parents are warmly presented in an easy-to-read book.

The Hundred Dresses, by Eleanor Estes. New York: Harcourt, 1944. 80p.

    THEME: Teasing of a child who is "different"

    AUDIENCE: Girls

READING LEVEL: Grade 4   INTEREST LEVEL: Ages 9–12

Wanda Petronski, a little Polish girl who lives way up on Boggins Heights, wears the same dress to school each day—a faded blue cotton dress, shabby but clean. Yet she says: "I got a hundred dresses home . . . all lined up in my closet." The other girls tease and ridicule her and do not understand until Wanda's family moves away and the girls learn that Wanda has won a prize for her colored drawings of a hundred dresses she would like to own.

A short but meaningful story to help girls to a better understanding of themselves and others. It should give pause for thought to all those who have ever inflicted mental cruelty, and could be reassuring to those who have been its victims. It could also help to overcome poor attitudes and relationships of children toward those who are "outside" their group.

Cathy's Secret Kingdom, by Nancy Faber. Philadelphia: Lippincott, 1963. 183p.

      THEME: Young girl's efforts to help her retarded stepsister
      AUDIENCE: Girls
READING LEVEL: Grades 4–5   INTEREST LEVEL: Ages 10–13

Cathy knows that houses aren't really haunted, but she is intrigued by the stories of the child crying in one of the bedrooms of a remodeled former church. Investigating, Cathy finds a place of her own, a secret kingdom, where she can write by herself. But she isn't alone for long, as Anne, her stepsister, suffering brain damage as a result of an accident, begs to be included. Through Cathy's efforts, Anne is brought out of her shell and accepted by her peers and her family.

Cathy's attempts to help her sister are part of an easy-reading, fast-moving story for girls. Anne is not a particularly strong character, but is illustrative of the loneliness of those who are ignored because they are "different."

Harriet the Spy, by Louise Fitzhugh. New York: Harper, 1964. 298p.

      THEME: Eleven-year-old girl's alienation of friends and classmates
      AUDIENCE: Girls
READING LEVEL: Grades 5–6   INTEREST LEVEL: Ages 10–14

Harriet wants to be a writer, and Ole Golly, her nurse, tells her that to succeed she should start writing things down. She also tells her to find out everything she can because "life is hard enough even if you know a lot." So Harriet becomes a spy, going on neighborhood expeditions where she observes people on her route, writing in her notebook observations and her inmost thoughts, whatever they may be. She also writes about her friends, classmates, and teachers. When Harriet's classmates find the notebook in which she has written uncomplimentary things about all of them, she becomes an outcast. This Harriet doesn't like, and she finally realizes that some truths must be left unsaid. So, as editor of the sixth-grade page of the school paper, she makes public apology for what she has written about her classmates.

There is material here for good guided discussion on peer relationships. Should friends say what they think of one another, or was Ole Golly right when she said, "Sometimes you have to lie"?

Whispering Willows, by Elisabeth Friermood. New York: Doubleday, 1964. 239p.

> THEME: Friendship between two girls of different races
> AUDIENCE: Girls
> READING LEVEL: Grade 7   INTEREST LEVEL: Ages 12 up

Tess Trumper, an orphan, lives with her Uncle Will, caretaker of the Willow Hill Cemetery. She helps him tend the graves and arranges flowers at the funerals. Her one dream is to become a horticulturist. A tall, serious girl, Tess finds most of her pleasures outside of school because she feels ill at ease with her classmates. Her best friend is a young black girl, Irene Washington. The two have played together, learned their ABCs together, and shared secrets since childhood. Irene becomes interested in a young man and marries him. Through this couple Tess shares in the early developments of the civil rights movement and in the joys and sorrows of Irene's large and generous family. Tess also comes to know herself better through Irene's gentle guidance.

This is a beautifully told story of the realistic friendship of two girls.

Jazz Country, by Nat Hentoff. New York: Harper, 1965. 146p.

> THEME: Breaking the color barrier
> AUDIENCE: Boys
> READING LEVEL: Grade 7   INTEREST LEVEL: Ages 12–17

During his senior year Tom Curtis devotes every spare moment to playing jazz on his trumpet. Drawn to the spots where really professional jazz is played, he hovers first on the periphery and finally moves into the inner circle of jazz players. His genuine talent presses him to make a difficult decision: has he "got the stuff" to succeed in a predominantly black art, "paying his dues" of struggle and search, or should he go to college, maybe "paying his dues" as a lawyer working on behalf of human rights?

This is an unusual, powerful novel, first as a story of jazz and how it shapes sounds from life and pain; second, as a study of prejudice in reverse, a white boy struggling to leap a color barrier; and finally, as a story of a teen-ager's soul-searching career choice. The stark, realistic rendering of emotions, the dialogue, and the abrasive encounters of blacks and whites will demand and hold attention.

From the Mixed-Up Files of Mrs. Basil E. Frankweiler, by Elaine L. Konigsburg. New York: Atheneum, 1967. 162p.

> THEME: Modern child seeking recognition
> AUDIENCE: Girls and boys

READING LEVEL: Grades 4–5   INTEREST LEVEL: Ages 9–12

Claudia feels that being the oldest in a family makes one subject to much injustice. To retaliate she runs away, choosing her nine-year-old brother Jamie as companion because "he keeps his mouth shut, he is good for a laugh sometimes, and he's rich." The two hide for a week in the Metropolitan Museum of Art in New York City, where they are intrigued by a lovely little statue whose origin baffles the experts. Claudia and Jamie decide to unravel the mystery, and in the process discover that they have become a team.

The author's good ear for the ordinary and her ability to create modern children makes this a notable family story.

Jennifer, Hecate, Macbeth, William McKinley, and Me, Elizabeth, by Elaine L. Konigsburg. New York: Atheneum, 1967. 117p.

> THEME: The friendship of two lonely girls
> AUDIENCE: Girls

READING LEVEL: Grade 5   INTEREST LEVEL: Ages 9–12

First spotted in a tree by Elizabeth, who tells the story, Jennifer blandly announces that she is a witch. Yes, she goes to school, but only to put the teacher under a spell. From that first meeting, the two become inseparable, just on Saturdays. It is on Saturdays that Jennifer instructs Elizabeth in the duties of an apprentice (later journeyman) witch. Elizabeth must follow some strange rules, such as never wearing shoes in the house on Sunday and eating a raw egg at least once a day for a week. But it is all worth it, for who else but a witch could produce watermelon in January? A flying ointment and a toad named Hilary Ezra break up the two for a time, but a very unwitchy Jennifer reappears and the two girls become what they really are—"just good friends."

This is a perceptive, yet childlike, account of two lonely children. Jennifer is the despair of her teachers, a loner who must manage things and people. She is searching for something else, however, and when she meets Elizabeth, the search for a friend comes to an end. Modern everyday "lingo" will make this a popular title with readers.

Meet the Austins, by Madeleine L'Engle. New York: Vanguard, 1960. 191p.

> THEME: Temporary disruption of the happy life of the Austins
> when a spoiled orphan joins them

AUDIENCE: Girls, possibly some boys
READING LEVEL: Grades 5–6   INTEREST LEVEL: Ages 10–14

The Austins, four children and their parents, are a gay, happy family when ten-year-old orphaned Maggy comes to live with them after her father dies in a plane crash. Maggy, an only child, is undisciplined and querulous, and soon upsets the happy atmosphere of the Austin home. Perceptive parents help their children to understand Maggy, and with love and discipline lead Maggy to controlled behavior. Events surrounding a visit from Uncle Douglas and a family vacation with Grandfather on a coastal island help bring mutual acceptance of Maggy and the Austins.

Told in the first person by twelve-year-old Vicky, the story reflects her adolescent emotions which lead to quarrels with an older brother. It is also bright with the warmth of family love, and the reader will perceive the qualities in human relationships which make them satisfying and happy.

Spring Begins in March, by Jean Little. Boston: Little, 1966. 156p.
  THEME: Friendship and good sibling relationship as an aid to self-
       discovery
  AUDIENCE: Girls
READING LEVEL: Grades 4–5   INTEREST LEVEL: Ages 9–11

Meg Copeland, youngest of her family, introduced in *Mine for Keeps,* is the protagonist in this story. Meg says: "I can't even have a little fun. . . . Whatever I do, somebody doesn't like it." At home her older sister, Sal, with whom she shares a room, complains of her disorderliness, and Grandmother, who has come to live with the family, complains of her general behavior. Her teacher complains of her inattention. A crisis is reached when Meg brings home a failing report card. Putting earlier friction aside, Sal and one of her friends step in to help by tutoring Meg every day after school. This help, an old diary of Grandmother's, and Grandmother's new interest in Meg combine to aid her in finding herself. Her acquisition of a puppy also figures in the story.

Family relationships are well portrayed, as is Meg's friendship with a classmate. Meg's counterparts in real life will readily identify with her.

Berries Goodman, by Emily Neville. New York: Harper, 1965. 178p.
  THEME: Encountering prejudice
  AUDIENCE: Boys and girls
READING LEVEL: Grade 5   INTEREST LEVEL: Ages 10–14

Berries Goodman and his family move from their cramped apartment in New York City to the suburbs so that they can have a back yard and a place for a dog. Instead of finding openness, Berries becomes enclosed by the walls of prejudice because of his relationship with Sidney Fine, a Jewish boy. They become good friends and enjoy bike riding, playing football, and just being together. Berries' next-door neighbor, Sandra, has acquired prejudice against Jews from her mother and resents the relationship of the boys. An accident in which Sidney is injured forces his parents to insist he not play with Berries. Believing this to be unfair, the boys defy their parents and meet secretly until discovered. Years later, when they are in high school and both have moved closer to New York, the boys renew their friendship to the surprise of their parents.

This story pulls no punches. Berries expresses it best when he asks, "How am I supposed to remember some kid is Jewish, when we're catching polliwogs or climbing a tree?" Prejudice is stripped bare, and the reader's emotions are not spared. An excellent book for discussion.

Second-hand Family, by Richard Parker. Indianapolis: Bobbs, 1966. 114p.
    THEME: Fitting into foster home
    AUDIENCE: Boys and girls
READING LEVEL: Grade 6   INTEREST LEVEL: Ages 11–16
Twelve-year-old orphaned Giles is sent to a new foster home, where he is told frankly that he is there merely because the family needs the money. Giles is anxious to really "belong," however, so he looks for the best in this wacky family. He gradually comes to like the gentle father, the tempestuous but understanding mother, offhand twelve-year-old Linda, and finally eighteen-year-old Martin, head of a combo. Martin resents having Giles as a roommate, but comes around after he helps the band to get its first job. A crisis is reached when it seems that Giles will have to return to the Home. Instead, the family decides to adopt Giles, proving to him that he has been accepted for himself.

Family Conspiracy, by Joan Phipson. New York: Harcourt, 1962. 224p.
    THEME: Children working to provide for mother's operation
    AUDIENCE: Boys and girls
READING LEVEL: Grade 5   INTEREST LEVEL: Ages 10–12
Four of the Barker children, Edward, Lorna, Robbie, and Belinda, realize that their mother needs an operation, and hospitals cost money. The children vow to earn as much as they can and to keep the project a secret from friends and parents; from Jack, a brother who is "too old"; and from sister Fanny, too young to know secrets. Unfortunately several of their schemes backfire. Robbie, for instance, is nearly killed when rotting timber in an old gold mine collapses. Tempers flare and actions are misunderstood by those not in on the "conspiracy."

Set on a sheep ranch in Australia, the Barkers could be any family, anyplace. They work against one another as often as not, but warmth and love and a depth of feeling are evident, even in blustering, bullying Mr. Barker.

The Egypt Game, by Zilpha Snyder. New York: Atheneum, 1967. 215p.
    THEME: Loneliness and creative friendship
    AUDIENCE: Girls and boys
READING LEVEL: Grade 5   INTEREST LEVEL: Ages 10–12
    April is a lonely little girl until she finds a friend in her neighbor Melanie, whose imagination is as vivid as April's own. The two girls recreate the land of ancient Egypt—Pharaoh, Osiris, oracle, and all—and with several recruits become completely involved in the ancient world until threatened by the violence of the modern one.
    The situation and characters are remarkably childlike. Conversations created by the author's ear for ordinary speech lack any self-consciousness, and the well-integrated "Egyptians"—black, Oriental, and "plain American"—are memorable children.

The Bully of Barkham Street, by Mary Stolz. New York: Harper, 1963. 194p.
    THEME: The relationships between a bully and his peers, and the reasons for them
    AUDIENCE: Boys and girls
READING LEVEL: Grades 4–5   INTEREST LEVEL: Ages 10–13
    Martin Hastings, large for his age, unhappy, at odds with family and peers, and with a quick temper, has the deserved reputation of being the local bully and fat boy of the small town where he lives. He is unable to maintain satisfactory relations with the only boy who makes overtures to him, and he bullies the boy next door, whose home life arouses Martin's envy. His sister and he fight and quarrel, each convinced that the other is the favorite child.
    After he starts to accept people as they are and does not always try to make excuses for his failures, Martin begins to establish friendlier relations with his peers and slowly makes his way out of "the bully's desert." By the end of the book, he has been accepted by his peers and his family, although the younger and older people of the community are not entirely convinced.
    The change in Martin is gradual, and there is much backsliding when everything does not go right, but this very slowness makes Martin's development all the more believable. The book could be used for discussions on bullies and why they act as they do.

The Noonday Friends, by Mary Stolz. New York: Harper, 1965. 182p.
    THEME: Family poverty and an eleven-year-old's home responsibilities which interfere with friendships
    AUDIENCE: Girls
READING LEVEL: Grade 5   INTEREST LEVEL: Ages 10–13

Franny Davis's artistic father has trouble holding a job, and in consequence her mother works outside the home. Franny's need for friendships is only partially satisfied because of her home responsibilities, and she feels humiliated by the fact that she must use a free lunch ticket at the school cafeteria. She fondly cares for Marshall, her little brother, after school, but her relationships with her twin brother, who has grown away from his family because of circumstances, lacks warmth. Friendships do blossom for Franny, partly with the help of a Puerto Rican youth who says that it takes compromise to make real friendships. Indirectly, through the same youth, Father eventually gets a job "he can stand."

The chapter telling of Marshall's fifth birthday celebration adds meaning to the book, for it conveys the feeling that those things done out of love are most meaningful. There is also reassurance for those who have trouble making friends.

Who Wants Music on Monday?, by Mary Stolz. New York: Harper, 1963. 264p.

  THEME: Members of a family unable to find a common ground
  AUDIENCE: Girls
  READING LEVEL: Grades 6–7   INTEREST LEVEL: Ages 13–16

Fourteen-year-old Cassie and her older brother and sister, Vincent and Lotta, are so different from one another that there is no genuine companionship and conversation between them. Cassie at first holds self-centered and conceited Lotta in contempt and clings to her understanding relationship with Vincent. During Lotta's senior year in high school the events of their lives give new perspective to each one's view of the others. None of them change radically, but they all gain a new appreciation of the others' ways of life and learn to accept one another as individuals.

A probing and introspective analysis of two sisters, who, although they occupy the same room, live in different worlds. Cassie constantly probes and rarely uses tact, while Lotta seems to float on the surface of life, secure in her ability to charm everyone she meets and giving the impression of never being touched by events around her. By the end of the story, Cassie has smoothed some of her rough edges and Lotta has learned the meaning of failure.

The Barrel, by Ester Wier. New York: McKay, 1966. 136p.

  THEME: Boy's finding of real courage
  AUDIENCE: Boys
  READING LEVEL: Grade 5   INTEREST LEVEL: Ages 10–14

When the welfare agency finally locates Chance Reedy's family, from whom he has been separated, Chance feels he will at last belong somewhere.

"Home" turns out to be a cottage on stilts in a Florida swamp, with super-stitious, lovable Granny and an older brother, Turpem, who is obsessed with proving his courage among the alligators, boars, and snakes. Turpem feels contempt for the shy puppy Chance chooses from his pack of terriers, and insists it must be put to the barrel test, being thrown into a barrel with a raccoon, as the Scots used to do with a badger. Granny wants the brothers to get along well, and frets that their father has passed on to Turpem his shallow, twisted concept of courage. A series of incidents proves Chance's mettle to himself and then to the others.

The book is quiet, understated, and powerful, similar in mood and ap-peal to the author's *The Loner.* The swamp country setting is especially well done.

Cathy's Little Sister, by Catherine Woolley. New York: Morrow, 1964. 190p.

THEME: The learning of independence through friendship

AUDIENCE: Girls

READING LEVEL: Grades 3–4   INTEREST LEVEL: Ages 8–12

At nine Chris has made no friends independently, but constantly trails her older sister, Cathy, and her friends. She even finds an excuse to stay home from school when Cathy is sick, and thus misses out on being in a class play. When Cathy has a slumber party and excludes Chris from the activities, she is crushed. On a subsequent overnight trip to Detroit with her father, Chris visits a home where she has a wonderful time with girls her own age. She also meets a little girl who trails her sister, even as she does, and begins to see herself as she is. Chris returns with plans for a slumber party of her own to which she will invite school classmates, and she is launched on a program of making friends of her own age.

An easy-to-read story, especially for girls who lack initiative in making friends of their own, and also for girls who cope with a "tag-along" sister.

Parents
with
Problems

. . . an answer to the critics who claim that books for and about young teen-agers ignore the real problems of today's society, idealize parents, and skirt sex, suicide and alcoholism.

RUTH HILL VIGUERS

Troublemaker, by Alberta Armer. Cleveland: World, 1966. 191p.

> THEME: Boy's adjustment to foster home when his own parents are unable to care for him
>
> AUDIENCE: Boys
>
> READING LEVEL: Grade 6   INTEREST LEVEL: Ages 11–14

Twelve-year-old Joe Fuller's father is in prison, and Joe is headed for trouble himself, having been apprehended for stealing a bicycle. When his mother is hospitalized for mental illness, Joe is sent to live in a foster home with the Murrays, who already have a foster daughter and two adopted children. Gradually Joe adjusts to the home, but continues in petty thievery, prompted by his wish to do something for his mother. When Joe hears that another foster child is to come into the home, he feels threatened, and steals money to run away. The understanding foster parents help Joe to see the error of his ways and to repay his debt. His mother's eventual recovery and the promise that his father will soon be released from prison give Joe hope for a reunited family of his own.

The characterization of Joe is good, his problems real, and his progressive adjustment believable. The hopeful ending could encourage the reader with similar home problems.

Queenie Peavy, by Robert Burch. New York: Viking, 1966. 159p.

> THEME: Girl with convict father develops sense of personal responsibility
>
> AUDIENCE: Girls and boys

94

READING LEVEL: Grades 5–6 INTEREST LEVEL: Ages 10–14

"Queenie's daddy's in the chain gang" echoes and re-echoes through the school yard, but thirteen-year-old Queenie feels sure that her dad will make everything right when he comes home. As the only girl in the eighth grade who can chew and spit tobacco, Queenie finds that her bad reputation gets her into trouble, even when she isn't directly to blame for the events in question. When Mr. Peavy is paroled, Queenie discovers that he isn't interested in her and that *she* must be responsible for her own actions.

Both city and country children who have known deprivation will identify with this spirited heroine.

A Breath of Fresh Air, by Betty Cavanna. New York: Morrow, 1966. 223p.

    THEME: Teen-age girl adjusting to parents' divorce

    AUDIENCE: Older girls

READING LEVEL: Grade 7 INTEREST LEVEL: Ages 12–17

Brooke Lawrence, high-school senior, is heartbroken when she learns that her parents are getting a divorce, and at first feels that her mother is being unfair to her father. Preparation of a term paper leads Brooke to do research on the life of Louisa May Alcott and her family. In the person of Bronson Alcott she sees reflected her own impractical father, and begins to have more insight into the incompatibility of her parents. By helping her mother with her business of selling antiques, Brooke gains more respect for her mother's abilities. As romance comes to her, Brooke examines her own philosophy of marriage. This adds value to the story.

A mature novel which should be helpful to young people trying to adjust to the divorce of parents.

The World of Ellen March, by Jeannette Eyerly. Philadelphia: Lippincott, 1964. 188p.

    THEME: Girl's attempt to reconcile divorced parents

    AUDIENCE: Girls

READING LEVEL: Grades 6–7 INTEREST LEVEL: Ages 12 up

Shocked when she hears of her parents' impending divorce, Ellen searches for ways to keep her family together. Her world shattered, unsure of herself, and almost friendless in a new school, she decides to "kidnap" her little sister and take her to a summer cottage where they cannot be found until the reunion of the family can take place. Events do not occur according to plan, and Ellen finds herself in a hospital with severe injuries. Although both parents do come to her bedside, as she had hoped, she is forced to realize that they will not live together again. With this realization she starts building a new life.

An excellent book for children from broken homes who blame themselves for the split, and who are unable to cope with the situation. Useful for discussion.

A Golden Touch, by Annabel and Edgar Johnson. New York: Harper, 1963. 230p.
>   THEME: Establishment of good father-son relationship
>   AUDIENCE: Boys

READING LEVEL: Grades 6–7   INTEREST LEVEL: Ages 11–15

Motherless Andy has the choice of going to an orphanage or joining his father, whom he hardly knows, in Colorado. With high hopes for adventure, Andy sets out for the Colorado gold mines, only to find his father in the hands of the sheriff and displeased at seeing him. Forced to leave town, Andy and his father are joined by Uncle Hep, and the three become involved in a run-down gold mine. Furtive movements and the strange behavior of his father reinforce Andy's suspicions that he is up to no good, though he badly wants to believe that his father is going straight. In a suspenseful climax the true villain is found, and Andy and his father set out together to seek their fortunes.

Camilla, by Madeleine L'Engle. New York: Crowell, 1965. 282p.
>   THEME: Parents' complication of their children's lives
>   AUDIENCE: Girls

READING LEVEL: Grade 7   INTEREST LEVEL: Ages 14 up

The bottom falls out of fifteen-year-old Camilla Dickinson's world when she discovers her adored, beautiful, overloving mother is having an illicit love affair. She clings to Luisa, a friend with quarrelsome, sometimes drunken parents, but it is in Luisa's brother Frank that Camilla finds strength, especially after Mrs. Dickinson's attempt to take her own life.

In spite of the subject, the story is neither harsh nor ugly. It is a sensitive story of a young girl's suffering, sorrow, and consequent maturity when faced with the complex and sometimes harrowing adult world.

The Unwilling Heart, by Catherine Marshall. New York: McKay, 1955. 245p.
>   THEME: A teen-age girl's acceptance of her father's imprisonment
>   AUDIENCE: Girls

READING LEVEL: Grades 6–7   INTEREST LEVEL: Ages 12–14

Linda is just back from a skiing trip when she hears of her father's imprisonment for embezzling. "I don't love him . . . I hate him," she cries. Trouble caused by a boy friend, and Linda's oversensitive reactions to overtures of sympathy, complicate her life until she comes to terms with herself.

Her father's difficulties point up Linda's own rather selfish outlook and help her develop more maturity and understanding.

Warmth and sympathetic understanding of a confused teen-ager make up for somewhat stilted conversations and formula plot in this readable junior novel. Will be helpful to girls with difficult parental problems.

To Shake a Shadow, by Phyllis R. Naylor. Nashville: Abingdon, 1967. 144p.

> THEME: Disturbance of boy whose father is in trouble with the law
> AUDIENCE: Boys

READING LEVEL: Grade 6 INTEREST LEVEL: Ages 11–15

When Brad Willson's father is caught in income tax evasion and is threatened with a term in prison, the shadow of family disgrace disrupts Brad's home life and fills him with rebellion. In his disturbed state, Brad is himself driven to petty thievery, and is tempted to join a gang given to vandalism and violence. An understanding school counselor and the friendship of a Jewish boy finally help Brad to come to terms with the situation and himself, and to accept the fact that he lives in a less-than-perfect world.

A fast-moving story which will hold the reader's interest, and one which may help readers to a better understanding of their own behavior, as well as that of others, under trying circumstances.

Jennifer, by Zoa Sherburne. New York: Morrow, 1959. 192p.

> THEME: Parent's drinking problem
> AUDIENCE: Girls

READING LEVEL: Grades 7–8 INTEREST LEVEL: Ages 12–17

In spite of Jennifer's happiness in her new home and the friends she makes at school, she fears that the good days will not last. She cannot bring herself wholly to trust that there will not be a recurrence of her mother's drinking which will destroy the family's hard-won peace and happiness. But when she sees that her mother has not only won her battle but can help others to do the same, Jennifer wins a battle of her own. She can now trust her mother and face the future with confidence.

This book can give hope to young people whose parents have had a drinking problem.

Stranger in the House, by Zoa Sherburne. New York: Morrow, 1963. 192p.

> THEME: A mother's return home after eight years in a mental institution
> AUDIENCE: Girls

READING LEVEL: Grade 6 INTEREST LEVEL: Ages 12–16

"Slowly encircling them, as relentlessly as a cold wind blowing through the warm and comfortable rooms, was the feeling of an alien presence, a stranger in the house." The alien presence, last remembered as a wildly deranged woman, is Mrs. Frazier, suddenly returned to her family after eight years in a mental institution. Her husband, her housekeeper, her young son Wimpy, and her daughter Kathleen, almost seventeen, wait on Mrs. Frazier, overprotect her, and treat her generally as a fragile lost soul, guarding her from work, noise, and people.

The gradual realization by the family that Mrs. Frazier is healed and ready to resume her wife-mother role is handled with sensitive attention to thoughts and emotions. The main focus is on Kathleen and the impact of her mother's return on her dating and school activities. Satisfying as a girls' story, this brief novel also achieves great strength as a study of people under stress.

A Tree Grows in Brooklyn, by Betty Smith. New York: Harper, 1943. 420p.

      THEME: Girl's relationship with alcoholic father

      AUDIENCE: Girls

READING LEVEL: Grade 8   INTEREST LEVEL: Ages 15 up

Francie Nolan loves her handsome Irish father, especially when he gets all dressed up for his job as a waiter with a fresh dicky and paper collar and sings "Molly Malone" in his clear voice. But her heart aches when he has to be helped home "sick." Johnny's drinking has caused the family to move twice and has taken its toll on him physically. Katie, his wife, tries to keep the household going with her three scrubbing jobs, but money is tight, and often there is little to eat and not enough fuel for warmth. Johnny is finally thrown out of the waiters' union because they consider him a bum and a drunk. This action is the fatal blow, and he dies three days later. Perseverance and an intense desire to get ahead help the remaining Nolans to pull themselves up by their bootstraps.

This is a warm family story filled with hardships, suffering, and tremendous obstacles, but most of all love, which can overcome a lot.

Miracles on Maple Hill, by Virginia Sorensen. New York: Harcourt, 1956. 180p.

      THEME: Family's year in the country as father recovers health

      AUDIENCE: Girls and boys

READING LEVEL: Grade 5   INTEREST LEVEL: Ages 10–13

Ten-year-old Marly, twelve-year-old Joe, and their parents move from the city to Maple Hill, Grandmother's Pennsylvania farm, hoping that "all outdoors" will help Father recuperate from his prisoner-of-war experiences. It is a time of adjustment, but also a year of revelation as Marly and Joe discover miracles in nature, and make friends with their new neighbors. Mr.

Chris, who owns a maple grove, is especially helpful to the family, and when he falls ill at sugaring time, they find in themselves new capabilities as they help save the crop. Father, whose returning health reassures and unites the family, works along with the rest.

The value of family cooperation in times of trouble and the restorative powers of nature are revealed in this book of spiritual worth.

The Long Ride Home, by James L. Summers. Philadelphia: Westminster, 1966. 170p.

    THEME: Alcoholic parent

    AUDIENCE: Boys and girls

READING LEVEL: Grade 7   INTEREST LEVEL: Ages 13–18

When the Blairs move to Paso Verde and Todd and Ann enroll at the town high school, they rebuff all overtures of friendship made by their new classmates. There is a reason. They are trying to keep up a front and to hide the fact of their father's alcoholism, not realizing that his condition cannot be hidden and has become common knowledge. Mother and children lead a miserable life until they are willing to share their problem with others. Todd finally attends an Alateen meeting for young people who have alcoholic relatives, but he does not accept their help. Finally, when Mr. Blair falls ill with alcoholic pneumonia and is in such desperate straits that he himself wants help, Alcoholics Anonymous can take over and the Blairs can look forward to a hopeful future.

A strongly written book that pulls no punches and strikes no false note. Should help young people in a similar situation to face facts and to see the need for help from the outside.

Good-bye to the Jungle, by John R. Townsend. Philadelphia: Lippincott, 1965. 184p.

    THEME: Children coping with poor home environment

    AUDIENCE: Boys and girls

READING LEVEL: Grade 7   INTEREST LEVEL: Ages 12–16

The "Jungle," a disintegrating neighborhood in an English city, is being leveled in a slum-clearance program, so the Thompsons are moving to Westwood, a suburban community. Here the children hope for a new life and new respectability. The head of the family, Walter Thompson, is given to spending his money (when he has any) on drink and gambling, and Doris, his lazy common-law wife, contributes little to a responsible way of life; so the young people take things into their own hands. Fifteen-year-old Kevin, who relates the story, and his fourteen-year-old sister had come to live with their uncle Walter when their parents died in an automobile accident. Pride, courage, and determination now spur their initiative to improve their way of life. They cannot change Walter or Doris, but they themselves develop a healthy set of values, and contribute to the development and welfare of their young cousins, one of whom is a genius.

A highly realistic story, with vivid characters, demonstrating that children can, to a degree at least, rise above a poor home environment.

Hostility and/or Problems
in Parent-Child
Relationships

Whatever the seeds of aggression may be in the child, we can help redirect these impulses into more wholesome avenues of expression.

ALLAN FROMME

Fifer for the Union, by Lorenzo Allen. New York: Morrow, 1964. 256p.

> THEME: Overcoming hostile feelings and rebellion against step-father
>
> AUDIENCE: Boys
>
> READING LEVEL: Grade 5   INTEREST LEVEL: Ages 10–14

The outbreak of the Civil War finds twelve-year-old Len missing his deceased father and rebelling with anger and impudence against his stepfather's discipline, mistaking guidance for tyranny. Len runs away from home, lies about his age, and is accepted into the Union fife and drum corps. Here he is befriended by a mature soldier, himself a stepfather, and through him Len comes to understand and respect his own stepfather as a trustworthy member of his family. Wartime experiences help Len to mature generally.

Large print may make this adventure story more inviting to reluctant readers. The book could give insight to boys who are hostile and rebellious over circumstances they do not fully understand, especially those with a stepfather problem.

That Jud!, by Elspeth Bragdon. New York: Viking, 1957. 126p.

> THEME: Orphan boy's proving his worth in the face of misunderstanding
>
> AUDIENCE: Boys and possibly some girls
>
> READING LEVEL: Grades 5–6   INTEREST LEVEL: Ages 10–14

In Spruce Point, Maine, where orphaned Jud is growing up, everyone

---

The titles in this section (except for *Smoke* by William Corbin McGraw) originally appeared in "The Hostile Child in Books," compiled and annotated by the Troubled Child Subcommittee, AHIL, American Library Association, in the September 1966 issue of *Exceptional Children.*

refers to him as "that Jud!" Sometimes it is said with affection, and sometimes with exasperation. Jud's frustrations, his loneliness, and sometimes his temper lead him into troubles such as truancy and window-breaking. In the course of his struggles to find satisfaction, Jud proves his worth to the community and gains self-respect when he risks his life to put out a dangerous fire.

Lonely and rebellious young people having trouble proving their worth to themselves and others may identify with Jud and be encouraged to find healthy outlets for their energies.

There Is a Tide, by Elspeth Bragdon. New York: Viking, 1964. 192p.

> THEME: Friction and rebellion stemming from the lack of close personal relationships
> AUDIENCE: Boys and girls
> READING LEVEL: Grades 5–6   INTEREST LEVEL: Ages 11–15

Nat Weston is motherless, and since his father is too absorbed in his work to show much interest in him, he feels friendless and alone. At fifteen Nat has been dismissed from numerous boys' schools as a troublemaker and a disturbing element. In telling of these years, beginning with an experience at eight when he was expelled and blamed for trouble for which he did not feel responsible, Nat says, "I went to the next school and the next and the next, fighting mad, hating everyone, and making as much trouble as I could." Now living with his father on an island off the coast of Maine, Nat has time for reflection, and here he has experiences and contacts (one with a girl who also has a chip on her shoulder) which help him to gain insight into his problems and to grow a little closer to his father. Soon he is ready to ask for another chance in school.

An absorbing story with convincing relationships and exciting action, this book should be especially helpful to readers who feel alone and filled with hatred and rebellion they do not understand. It could also encourage better father-son relationships and a greater sense of responsibility.

Big Blue Island, by Wilson Gage. New York: World, 1964. 120p.

> THEME: Anger and rebellion over domestic problems
> AUDIENCE: Boys and possibly some girls
> READING LEVEL: Grade 5   INTEREST LEVEL: Ages 9–12

Desertion and death rob eleven-year-old Darrell of his parents, and he is an angry, rebellious boy when he comes to live with his great-uncle on a lonely Tennessee River island. He misses city activities and feels marooned on the island without electricity, television, or radio. To make matters worse, Darrell mistakes his uncle's independent spirit for indifference, and he feels unwanted. As his anger gradually gives way to fascination with the island's wild life, especially the heron, Darrell's respect for his uncle grows, and the story comes to a hopeful conclusion.

A sullen, indifferent boy might well identify with Darrell and gain insight into relative values. The author's appreciation of nature could be contagious, and the reader might sense that things worth having are not always readily apparent.

Gull Number 737, by Jean George. New York: Crowell, 1964. 198p.

THEME: Rebellion of teen-ager against image his father has of him
AUDIENCE: Boys and perhaps girls
READING LEVEL: Grades 6–7   INTEREST LEVEL: Ages 11–16

After many years of assisting his father in a study of seagulls, sixteen-year-old Luke suddenly finds his father dull, arbitrary, and tyrannical, and his work tedious and impractical. Confused and guilt-ridden, Luke keeps his feelings of disloyalty and rebellion to himself until an episode concerning the crash of a jet airliner brings his father into the limelight. This provides Luke with an opportunity to defy him openly and involve himself in original, scientific work on his own.

Teen-agers will find valuable this example of a natural growth pattern which many find a problem. They will see that increasing maturity and the desire to follow one's own goals necessitate an alteration in father-son relationships.

The Grizzly, by Annabel and Edgar Johnson. New York: Harper, 1964. 160p.

THEME: Boy's overcoming fear caused by demanding father
AUDIENCE: Boys and fathers
READING LEVEL: Grade 5   INTEREST LEVEL: Ages 10–14

Fear permeates all memories eleven-year-old David has of his father, a capable outdoorsman who expects similar fearlessness in his son. Mark, the father, returns after a long separation and uses his court-awarded visiting privileges to take Dave on a camping trip. Nearly paralyzed by the fear that his father will abandon him in the wilderness as a test, David becomes more bumbling and withdrawn than ever. Fear soon turns into hatred. But a gallant fight with a grizzly reveals the protectiveness and kindliness in Mark and enables Dave to discover that he is tenacious and resourceful, despite his underdeveloped physical ability.

This book is readable, exciting, terse, and could be useful with overprotected, fearful, unconfident, and lonely children whose fathers tend to attempt to mold their sons in their own images.

Torrie, by Annabel and Edgar Johnson. New York: Harper, 1960. 217p.

    THEME: Girl's selfish lack of understanding of her parents

    AUDIENCE: Girls and possibly a few boys

READING LEVEL: Grades 6–7   INTEREST LEVEL: Ages 12–16

    Fourteen-year-old Torrie is reluctant to leave her comfortable Saint Louis home to join her family on a hazardous covered-wagon trip to California. Her selfish, antagonistic attitude toward her parents results in a misunderstanding of their motives in undertaking the trip. The wagon train meets with many reverses: illness, Indian attacks, hunger, and dissension among its members. Torrie learns to respect her parents when she recognizes the bravery and selflessness which make them true leaders. Love for a young man who also gives freely of himself helps Torrie to mature and accept new values.

    Torrie could suggest to its readers what true adulthood and parenthood involve—mature acceptance of responsibility for the good of all. It could also promote an understanding of and need for discipline.

Onion John, by Joseph Krumgold. New York: Crowell, 1959. 248p.

    THEME: Father-son conflict; ignoring of individual differences and rights

    AUDIENCE: Boys and possibly some girls

READING LEVEL: Grades 5–6   INTEREST LEVEL: Ages 10–15

    Andy Rusch, at twelve, lives in the small town of Serenity and develops a close friendship with an eccentric old immigrant, Onion John, who lives in a crude stone house he himself built on nearby Hessian Hill. Onion John's superstitions, happy kindliness, and irregular way of life captivate Andy and his peers and stir benevolence in the hearts of the townspeople. But when the latter try to change and improve John's casual way of living, they almost destroy him. In the process, Andy and his father both grow, Andy into a more mature youth and his father to a greater understanding of himself and his son, in whom he had been hoping to realize his own thwarted ambitions.

    This is a very perceptive story written in the first person and with language, feeling, and action meaningful to the adolescent boy. The father-son conflict and its happy resolution make this a book not only for the adolescent boy whose father has planned his life for him without any thought to the boy's own interests, but for the father as well.

The Rock and the Willow, by Mildred Lee. New York: Lothrop, 1963. 223p.

    THEME: Unhappy home conditions, poverty, and loss of mother as they affect a girl's plans for the future

AUDIENCE: Girls
READING LEVEL: Grade 7   INTEREST LEVEL: Ages 13–18

Enie, the eldest daughter of a dirt farmer in Georgia during the depression, starts to dream of going to college when her teachers praise her writing talent. Her father subordinates everything to the good of his farm, and his dictatorial ways drive his son away. The mother dies the night of Enie's
• graduation from high school, and her father marries a woman whom Enie dislikes. However, it is through this woman that she has the chance to go to college.

The relationship between parents and children in a poor family and the reactions toward a father who runs his family with a heavy hand are familiar to many children. Enie's story might offer new ways of coping with such unpleasant home situations.

Smoke, by William Corbin McGraw. New York: Coward, 1967. 253p.
    THEME: Growing respect for and acceptance of stepfather
    AUDIENCE: Boys
READING LEVEL: Grade 6   INTEREST LEVEL: Ages 10–14

Chris Long finds it next to impossible to accept his new stepfather, and often seeks refuge from his hostile feelings in a tree house on a mountainside above the family's Oregon farm. From this site he first sees a German Shepherd dog, turned wild, and determines to tame and make a pet of him. He finally succeeds, only to have the dog's real owner turn up. To avoid giving up the dog, and to escape an unacceptable home situation, Chris runs away with him. As the result of a fracas between his dog and another, Chris is injured. During the treatment of his wounds, many things from his past life run through his mind, and he emerges a more mature person, ready to return home and to accept his stepfather.

A moving story of a boy and the dog he comes to love, and of his improving relationship with his stepfather. An aspect of the story which might add to its usefulness is the fact that Chris conquers a fear of darkness during his night alone in the mountains.

It's Like This, Cat, by Emily Neville. New York: Harper, 1963. 180p.
    THEME: The lack of communication and understanding between a
           boy and his father
    AUDIENCE: Boys
READING LEVEL: Grades 5–6   INTEREST LEVEL: Ages 12–15

Dave Mitchell's resentment of his father, though not violent, is deep-seated. Every conversation between them ends in misunderstanding and confusion. Through the wanderings of Cat, a pet chosen because Mr. Mitchell likes dogs, Dave meets Tom Ransom, a college dropout. To Dave's amazement, Tom turns to Mr. Mitchell for help and advice, and, as Dave observes his father helping the young man to regain his self-respect and ambition, he grows to understand his father better and to appreciate his good qualities.

Parents and children often find it difficult to understand each other, and this lucid treatment of the subject could open the way for discussion of misunderstandings in these relationships.

Fisherman's Choice, by Elsa Pedersen. New York: Atheneum, 1964. 182p.
> THEME: Teen-ager's attempt to become a man, despite stifling mother love
> AUDIENCE: Boys and possibly girls
> READING LEVEL: Grade 7 INTEREST LEVEL: Age 12–16

In an attempt to earn enough money to help support his family's Alaskan homestead, seventeen-year-old Dave accepts the only available job open to boys under eighteen—a hand on a fishing boat. He and the captain's nephew, Tommy, react violently to each other, and Dave nearly loses his life through the other boy's extreme jealousy. His decision to remain a fisherman and abandon homesteading results in violent family reaction, for his mother views this as a disintegration of her carefully sheltered family, rather than as a natural desire for independence.

Dave's growth and maturity, as reflected in his thinking, actions, and decisions, form the heart of the book. Because his affection for his family is deep and genuine, his decision to seek his own place in the sun, an instinctively right one, takes real courage. The subplot involves similar problems of his sister's.

The Bronze Bow, by Elizabeth Speare. Boston: Houghton, 1961. 255p.
> THEME: Hatred and the seeking of revenge
> AUDIENCE: Girls and boys
> READING LEVEL: Grades 7–8 INTEREST LEVEL: Ages 12–16

Based on biblical history, this is the story of a boy's struggle with the forces of hatred and rebellion during the early Christian era when Galilee was under Roman rule. Having witnessed the murder of his parents by Romans, Daniel vows vengeance, joining an outlaw band dedicated to the overthrow of the Romans. Involving his friends in the dangers of aggressive activity, Daniel gradually becomes disillusioned with violence and the outlaw band and succumbs to the law of love being preached in Galilee by the rabbi Jesus.

This forceful novel's message of the power of love over hate seems especially pertinent in today's world. The author's purpose, to provide a positive philosophy of life that will give meaning where emptiness has prevailed, could well be realized in teen-age readers.

Perilous Road, by William Steele. New York: Harcourt, 1958. 191p.
    THEME: Boy's misunderstanding of parental attitudes
    AUDIENCE: Boys and girls
READING LEVEL: Grade 5   INTEREST LEVEL: Ages 10–14
    Young Chris Brabson, living in Tennessee during Civil War days, hates the Yankees because some have plundered his home. He finds it hard to understand how his brother can join the Union army or why his parents take no stand for either side. When Chris undertakes aggressive action on his own against Union forces and meets Union men, he comes to the surprised realization that a Union soldier may be a "good decent man" with needs and interests akin to his own.

    Through this fast-paced story, the reader may gain wisdom and insight into the relative importance of life's values. The book could especially help an impulsive person to consider the dangers of aggression based on hatred. Some Southern dialect may make reading difficult.

The Bully of Barkham Street, by Mary Stolz. New York: Harper, 1963. 194p.
    THEME: The motivations of a bully's actions
    AUDIENCE: Boys
READING LEVEL: Grades 4–5   INTEREST LEVEL: Ages 9–14
    Martin is larger and older than any of his classmates. His sense of frustration at this is evidenced by a surly attitude toward adults, distrust of friendly overtures, and the bullying of younger boys. His one love is his dog, and when the dog is removed because of Martin's repeated fights, his problems are intensified. Martin's slow road back to acceptance by his peers and adults is far from smooth.

    Martin's attitudes toward others, his desire to be accepted, and his fight within himself to do what he knows is right make him a sympathetic person and provide a better understanding of the reasons behind a bully's behavior. This book follows *Dog on Barkham Street,* which shows the antagonism of the community to the same boy.

Trouble Creek, by Jo Sykes. New York: Holt, 1963. 217p.
    THEME: Teen-age boy's resentment of new stepfather
    AUDIENCE: Boys
READING LEVEL: Grades 6–7   INTEREST LEVEL: Ages 12–16
    Ten Holland's jealousy of his stepfather, Dick, causes him to misconstrue Dick's actions, and his hostile attitude brings out the testier aspects of his

stepfather's personality. Stepfather and son serve as guides for Lantis Brighton and his son George, who are on a wilderness search for a lost son and brother presumed dead. During this unhappy search, Ten witnesses another regrettable father-son relationship which sheds light on his own problem. The latter relationship forms a substantial subplot which revolves around the favorite-son theme. The problems of the Brightons and the demands of the wilderness enable all characters to re-evaluate themselves.

The World for Jason, by Marguerite Vance. New York: Dutton, 1961. 150p.

    THEME: Father-son conflict over boy's choice of vocation

    AUDIENCE: Boys and possibly some girls

READING LEVEL: Grade 5   INTEREST LEVEL: Ages 9–13

Jason, whose father is an aerialist with the circus, lives in a world of conflict. His father, the Great Rudolph, stubbornly insisting that Jason follow him in his circus career, is blind to his son's fear of high places and his marked talent for the piano. Jason's uncle, a wild-animal trainer, gives the boy affection and understanding and serves as a buffer in the father-son conflict. Reluctantly, Rudolph assents to Jason's going to New York to live with maternal relatives and receive musical training. The gulf between father and son is gradually bridged, and when Jason makes his debut at Carnegie Hall, his encore is his own composition interpreting his father's life as an aerialist. As he responds to the applause, he knows that he has found a way to express love for his father while using his best talents.

The story makes real the fact that love and conflict can live side by side and that, if love is strong enough, it will break the barriers of differences. Here is a message for both fathers and sons whose talents and interests tend to set them apart. Adding interest to the story is a circus-born panther raised by Jason, which later turns upon everyone except the boy.

Nature Books
for Release
of Tension

Know, man hath all which Nature hath, but more,
And in that more lie all his hopes of good.
                                        MATTHEW ARNOLD

Horns of Plenty, by Jane and Paul Annixter. New York: Holiday House, 1960. 203p.

    THEME: Boy's achievement of understanding that matches his courage

    AUDIENCE: Boys

READING LEVEL: Grade 5   INTEREST LEVEL: Ages 11–16

    As a hunter's guide Garry Luckett knows the rims and ravines of the Rockies, the track of the grizzly and horseshoe rabbit, the flight of the bald eagle, the stealth of the cougar, and most of all the magnificent stance of the king ram Big Eye. Promised a thousand-dollar reward for "the horns of plenty" which grace the sheep's head, Garry goes in search of the animal. He is twice attacked by a killer cougar and shares hibernation quarters with a grizzly before he at last finds Big Eye.

    In Garry the reader meets a boy of high physical courage who nurtures an inner resentment toward his father. Even as he tracks a dangerous animal, Gary finds himself blaming his parent for unkept promises and impracticality. It takes a bookful of nerve-tingling adventures before Gary achieves understanding to match his courage.

Castaway Christmas, by Margaret J. Baker. New York: Farrar, 1963. 158p.

    THEME: Cooperation brought about in mastering a flood

    AUDIENCE: Boys and girls

READING LEVEL: Grades 5–6   INTEREST LEVEL: Ages 10–12

    The Ridley children—seventeen, fifteen, and ten years of age—plan to meet their traveling parents at a rented house in the country for Christmas.

Upon arrival at the house they discover that their parents have been delayed and that there is very little food. The heavy rains which have been falling soon cause floods which isolate the house completely from sources of food and heat. The struggles of the three to survive the elements and to exist with one another are very credible. They bicker and fight as brothers and sisters do, and not until they are faced with the rescue of a neighbor's wife, child, and sheep do they start to work together. When their parents arrive on Christmas Day, all is again under control.

The book is a good study of three very normal children under the stress of hunger, cold, and flood. Their courage and bravery are set against a background of discouragement, worry, and homesickness and are thus more admirable.

Pinto's Journey, by Wilfrid S. Bronson. New York: Messner, 1948. 57p.

      THEME: The courage to overcome wild animals, engendered by concern for the family

      AUDIENCE: Boys and girls

READING LEVEL: Grade 4   INTEREST LEVEL: Ages 9–11

Pinto, a Pueblo Indian boy, living with his mother and grandfather during war years when the young men are away fighting for their country, is challenged by Grandfather's need for turquoise for making jewelry. Without jewelry to trade, the family would soon starve. Wishing to be helpful, Pinto takes the burro, his bow and arrow, and Grandfather's hammer, and sets out to find the secret mines he has heard Grandfather describe. The trail is difficult, and wild animals a hazard, but Pinto bests a bear and a mountain lion in his successful mission to bring back turquoise in time for the Christmas fiesta.

A colorfully illustrated modern Indian adventure with exciting wild-animal encounters in rugged terrain. Courage like Pinto's is something for which youth may well strive.

The Incredible Journey, by Sheila Burnford. Boston: Little, 1961. 145p.

      THEME: How courage, teamwork, and persistence overcome great odds

      AUDIENCE: Boys and girls

READING LEVEL: Grades 5–6   INTEREST LEVEL: Ages 11 up

A Labrador retriever, an old bull terrier, and a Siamese cat belonging to the Hunter family are boarded with a friend while their owners are away on a trip. Left unguarded, the three set out on a 250-mile journey, mostly through uninhabited territory, to find their masters. In spite of their dissimilarities, they form a close team under the retriever's leadership. Their eagerness to get home is such that they surmount incredible barriers.

The story of the animals' struggles against swollen streams, hills, and trackless forests is a compelling one. Each of the animals becomes a personality distinct from the others, and the writing is such that the reader becomes closely involved with their efforts. A marvelous story of courage, teamwork, and persistence in the face of overwhelming odds.

Wild Boy, by Thomas Fall. New York: Dial, 1965. 105p.
    THEME: Physical courage coupled with reverence for life
    AUDIENCE: Boys
READING LEVEL: Grade 5   INTEREST LEVEL: Ages 10 up

Roberto, living in West Texas in the 1870s, sees his father and grandfather die in attempts to capture Diablo Blanco, the wildest mustang in the Southwest. To avenge their deaths, Roberto persuades a Comanche chief, a friend of his grandfather, to permit him to train for mustang capturing in a Comanche camp. Armed with this training as well as his own courage and resourcefulness, Roberto finally accomplishes the near-impossible feat of capturing Diablo Blanco. In so doing he builds up such admiration for the proud wild creature that he refuses the thousand-dollar bounty when he knows the mustang will be crippled by the new owner. His compassion for men as well as animals is evidenced when he performs a courageous act to save many lives threatened by war.

Although set in a past century, this moving story has a message for today. Courage, coupled with a "reverence for life" and freedom, characterize the hero, who thinks: "If people used as much imagination to prevent war as they spend in waging it . . . they might indeed be of a higher order than animals."

Vulpes, the Red Fox, by John and Jean George. New York: Dutton, 1948. 184p.
    THEME: A fox's facing a hostile world
    AUDIENCE: Boys and girls
READING LEVEL: Grades 5   INTEREST LEVEL: Ages 10–12

Vulpes, a red fox who roamed the hills of Virginia, becomes a real personality in this book by two outstanding nature writers. His growing up, his maturing, his outwitting of his enemies, and the final hunt are full of nature lore and a feel of the out-of-doors.

In this story of a courageous animal, boys can identify themselves with the clever and resourceful fox and with his efforts to make a life for himself in a hostile world where he constantly hunts and is hunted.

Old Yeller, by Fred Gipson. New York: Harper, 1956. 158p.
  THEME: A boy's growth to maturity in wild hill country
  AUDIENCE: Boys and girls
READING LEVEL: Grade 6   INTEREST LEVEL: Ages 11–16
  At fourteen Travis is left "man of the family" at his Texas ranch home while his father goes to Kansas to sell cattle. Having recently lost a beloved dog, Travis does not at first take kindly to the big yellow dog that shows up at the ranch one morning, stealing a side of pork. Little brother Arliss immediately loves and adopts the dog, which the family names Old Yeller. Later, when the dog saves Arliss's life as he is threatened by an angered mother bear, Travis looks upon him with growing affection. When Old Yeller proves himself valuable in countless ways, Travis realizes that he cannot carry on as "man of the family" without him. Finally, while saving Travis's mother from a mad wolf, Old Yeller is bitten by the wolf, and Travis is forced to shoot the beloved dog.
  Travis grows in maturity as he experiences the pains of life along with its pleasures.

Stormy, Misty's Foal, by Marguerite Henry. Chicago: Rand McNally, 1963.
    THEME: Community cooperation in the face of natural disaster
    AUDIENCE: Boys and girls
READING LEVEL: Grade 5   INTEREST LEVEL: Ages 10–12
  Misty, a pony so famous she's been in the movies, is a prime worry of Paul and Maureen Beebe. As Grandma Beebe says, "A storm's a-brewing," and Misty is about to foal. The terror of the storm that descends on Chincoteague Island, where the Beebes live, forces them to leave Pony Ranch, Misty, and Grandma's herd of ponies. High water and gale winds kill many of the animals, but Misty manages to survive, and her colt is born after the storm.
  The story of Stormy and Misty and the herding of wild ponies on Chincoteague and Assateague Islands is based on actual fact. In a spontaneous show of interest, children of the community name Stormy and also send pennies to rebuild the herd. This joint effort indicates that no one stands completely alone in time of disaster.

Burma Boy, by Willis Lindquist. New York: McGraw-Hill, 1953. 96p.
    THEME: How fearlessness born of love can overcome great obstacles
    AUDIENCE: Boys and girls
READING LEVEL: Grades 4–5   INTEREST LEVEL: Ages 9–12
  Haji, son of a disabled elephant rider and trainer for the Rangoon Rubber Company, has loved and played with his father's huge elephant, Majda

Koom, since early childhood. Now, with his master gone from the scene where he had worked, Majda Koom has returned to the jungle and become a wild killer. Some of the natives think him mad from grief for his master, and when he appears again in the villages with a herd of wild elephants, endangering life and property, they seek to kill him. Fearlessness and courage, born of love for the great elephant, make possible Haji's tracking down and once more gentling his old friend.

Author and artist combine their talents to make this book a vivid, dramatic excursion into the Burmese jungle. The tense moments hold the reader to the very end, where he will live Haji's success with him.

The Call of the Wild, by Jack London. New York: Macmillan, 1903, 1956. 142p.

THEME: Kindness can tame even the wild

AUDIENCE: Boys and girls

READING LEVEL: Grades 6–8   INTEREST LEVEL: Ages 12 up

Buck, part Saint Bernard dog, part wolf, is snatched from his comfortable home in California to pull sleds for gold seekers during the Alaskan Gold Rush. At first resentful of his rough treatment, Buck lashes out against his human captors, but he quickly learns the rule of the club. The dogs he works with are little better than wild, and by observation he learns what happens to the weak and timid ones. He becomes the strongest dog in his team and proves his worth over and over in strange and hostile surroundings where snow, ice, and storm are the normal conditions. When a careless handler leaves him on the brink of death, he is saved by the only man who gains his affection. He is now so wild that he increasingly responds to the call of the wild wolves who roam the countryside. When his master is killed by Indians, his last link with civilized life is gone, and he becomes the undisputed and much feared leader of the pack, never to return to the life he has known.

Buck's story, with its portrayal of the harsh and cruel elements of life, is an exciting and moving one, filled with courage in the face of great odds. The rewards of kindness are seen in Buck's response to the man who befriends him.

Lost in the Barrens, by Farley Mowat. Boston: Little, 1956. 244p.

THEME: Courage when confronted with the struggle for survival

AUDIENCE: Boys

READING LEVEL: Grade 5   INTEREST LEVEL: Ages 10–15

When starvation threatens a Cree village, Chief Meewasin organizes a hunting expedition to seek caribou. His son, Awasin, and Jamie Macnair, nephew of an Indian trader, are allowed to go along. As they go farther north the chief decides to scout ahead and leaves the two boys at a base camp in the care of two Indians. Bored, they decide to explore on their own, but through a freak accident are cut off from all contact with both parties. Their only hope for survival is to prepare for the coming winter and hold out until help arrives. With Jamie's ingenuity and Awasin's knowledge of the wilderness, they withstand bitter storms and a monotonous existence until rescued by the once-dreaded Eskimos.

This Canadian-Arctic adventure portrays the courage man finds within himself when confronted with the struggle for survival. The fact that the feat was accomplished by two young boys adds to the appeal of this exciting book.

Silver Chief, Dog of the North, by Jack O'Brien. New York: Holt, 1933. 218p.

> THEME: Devoted friendship between a Mountie and his dog in the wild north country
>
> AUDIENCE: Boys and girls

READING LEVEL: Grades 5-6   INTEREST LEVEL: Ages 10 up

Silver Chief, son of a wild huskie and a wolf, learns from his mother to hunt for food and to beware of man. Seeing her killed by an Indian makes him hate all men. Then Sergeant Jim Thorne of the Canadian Northwest Mounted Police pursues a murder suspect into the area where Silver Chief roams and hunts. He sees the dog and becomes determined to capture him for a friend and as leader of his huskies. After many trials, Jim succeeds, and a warm devotion develops between the two. When the murder suspect ambushes Jim and shoots him in the leg, Silver Chief attacks the suspect and makes him a prisoner. Aided by the dog, Jim forces the prisoner to care for him until a lull in the weather makes it possible to attempt a trip to headquarters.

Though Jim suffers and displays great courage, the story belongs to Silver Chief. His strength, tenderness, and loyalty are qualities worthy of emulation. Readers will identify with both Silver Chief and Jim in their struggles against the elements of nature and evil.

Island of the Blue Dolphins, by Scott O'Dell. Boston: Houghton, 1960. 184p.

> THEME: Survival on a deserted island
>
> AUDIENCE: Boys and girls

READING LEVEL: Grade 6   INTEREST LEVEL: Ages 11-13

Karana, a young Indian girl living on an island off the coast of Lower California, sees her father and the strongest men of the tribe killed by Aleutian seal hunters. The remainder of the tribe is evacuated by ship to the mainland, but Karana and her younger brother are left behind. The brother is killed by wild dogs who roam the island, and Karana is left to fend for herself. At first sure of rescue and then more and more adjusted to her solitary life, she lives by her own ingenuity for eighteen long years. She befriends the leader of the pack of wild dogs for companionship, tames a young seal, and, through hard work and her knowledge of the island, outwits Aleutian seal hunters. She survives cold, hunger, and an earthquake until the day she is rescued.

Based on the life of an Indian girl rescued from just such an island in the 1800s, this is the moving story of a girl's survival and refusal to admit defeat. The details of her methods of obtaining shelter, food, and clothing are fascinating and vivid, and her indomitable spirit evokes a strong empathy in the reader.

Dingo, by Mary Patchett. New York: Doubleday, 1963. 156p.
    THEME: Boy's affection for a wild dog
    AUDIENCE: Boys
READING LEVEL: Grade 6   INTEREST LEVEL: Ages 12–18

In the still-wild outreaches of Australia, land of goannas and kangaroos, Small McLean befriends a forlorn wild pup. Aware that there is a bounty on the baby dingo, predator of cattle and sheep, the little boy finds a sanctuary cave for the animal and cares for Mirri until the dog's instincts send him forth almost grown to the ways of the wild.

Again and again the paths of boy and wild dog meet and part. No trap, no bullet is enough to take Mirri's life because Small McLean is always there to save him. Finally it is Mirri who saves the boy's life in a fire and sacrifices his own chance for survival.

A splendid picture of Australian wildlife and of boy-dog devotion.

Boundary Riders, by Joan Phipson. New York: Harcourt, 1962. 189p.
    THEME: Surmounting disaster with courage
    AUDIENCE: Boys and girls
READING LEVEL: Grade 5   INTEREST LEVEL: Ages 10–13

Jane and Bobby Thompson, together with their trustworthy fifteen-year-old cousin, Vincent, set out on a camping trip to inspect boundary fences of the newly acquired Thompson ranch in Australia. They take with them supplies to last a week, and having finished their inspection with three days to spare, they decide to explore, searching for a beautiful waterfall they have glimpsed from a distance. Caught in a heavy mist following a storm, they become lost and are thrown into harrowing experiences in rough terrain. A dog, whom Bobby rescues from a deserted mine, finally leads them to a lonely farm dwelling. Here they are further challenged by a seemingly impossible river crossing, made imperative by severe illness. Bobby meets the challenge, finds a way, and effects rescue for his party and their new friends.

The story is notable not only for its vivid recounting of young people's surmounting disaster, but for the emerging personality of Bobby, whose courage matches his challenge.

Daughter of the Mountains, by Louise Rankin. New York: Viking, 1948. 191p.

> THEME: Girl's searching for her dog with perseverance, faith, and courage
> AUDIENCE: Girls and some boys

READING LEVEL: Grades 5–6   INTEREST LEVEL: Ages 10–14

Momo prays to her Buddhist idols for a red-gold Lhasa terrier like the one belonging to the head lama of the monastery. No sooner is she given the terrier, Pempa, than he is spirited away by a thieving trader in a mule train. On a pilgrimage to find her dog, Momo sets forth alone from her village in the Jelep La Pass of Tibet. Down, down the mountain, through strange villages and across terrain now beautiful, now desolate, Momo follows the Great Trade Route from Tibet through Sikkim to India and at last to the highly populated metropolis of Calcutta, where her search ends.

This is a story made rich by the faith and courage of a little girl, the wondrous beauty of mountains and wild creatures and the discovery of things she has never before seen. A child who has loved a pet, or any child who wonders if dreams can come true, will join Momo in her search.

The Yearling, by Marjorie Rawlings. New York: Scribner, 1939. 405p.

> THEME: A boy's ability to relinquish as a sign of maturity
> AUDIENCE: Boys and girls

READING LEVEL: Grade 7   INTEREST LEVEL: Ages 12 up

Jody Baxter, only son of hardworking parents living in wild, beautiful Florida country, shares his father's love of nature and creatures of the wild. His mother, hardened by years of reverses, frowns upon Jody's wish for a pet, and only through an accident does he finally acquire a fawn. For a time the fawn dominates his whole life, and the two are inseparable. Then the growing fawn destroys crops which are the family's livelihood, and even while resisting, Jody realizes that the fawn must go. The heartbreaking parting sends the boy into deep despair, but eventually also helps him to grow up emotionally.

Although long, this is rewarding reading for young people, many of whom can identify with Jody in one way or another. The story stirs within the reader a gamut of emotional feelings as Jody progresses from childhood and becomes a man. Violence in nature, and successful conquest thereof, could mean important emotional release for the reader.

The Blind Colt, by Glen Rounds. New York, Holiday, 1941. unp.
> THEME: Survival of a blind wild colt
> AUDIENCE: Boys and girls
READING LEVEL: Grade 5   INTEREST LEVEL: Ages 10–16

In the rain-gullied buttes of the Badlands a colt is born frisky and curi-
ous like all colts, except for one thing—he is blind. Young Whitey and
his Uncle Torwal spot the animal when they ride out to check their range
stock, and Uncle Torwal thinks it best to shoot the colt. When Whitey begs
for his life, however, he is left to run free. Through the changing of the
seasons the colt learns the smell and sound and shape of danger in rattle-
snakes, gullies, sucking mud, and wolves. When a blizzard threatens his
life, the blind colt finds his way to Uncle Torwal's stable and to Whitey's
gentling, taming hands.

This very special story will win boys with its brevity, its portrait of an
animal struggling for survival, and its boy-beast friendship.

Avalanche!, by A. Ruthers van der Loeff. New York: Morrow, 1958.
219p.
> THEME: A boy's struggle in the face of death-dealing avalanches
> AUDIENCE: Boys and girls
READING LEVEL: Grade 5   INTEREST LEVEL: Ages 10–16

An Alpine town is entombed in deadly white snow. Young Werner, the
schoolmaster's son, burrows his way out of the wreckage that was his home
and is evacuated, leaving his parents somewhere in the debris. By the time
he learns that his parents have been saved, he has changed from a solitary,
uncommunicative boy to a young man ready to work in the Children's Village, a center for war orphans.

This novel demands taut attention with its authentic picture of people
who live and die in a land of melting mountainsides which can be triggered
into action by a breath of wind. Just as real as nature's trickery are the
joyous new friendships which soon bind Werner and the young refugees of
the international village together. The children prove to Werner that "you're
only happy if you *know* you're happy. And you only know that after you've
been miserable."

Hill's End, by Ivan Southall, New York: St. Martin's, 1963. 174p.
> THEME: Seven children face the problem of survival in their de-
> stroyed town
> AUDIENCE: Boys and girls
READING LEVEL: Grades 6–7   INTEREST LEVEL: Ages 11–16

On the island of Tasmania the townspeople of Hill's End go for an
annual outing to Stanley, eighty-five miles away. This year seven of the
children, ages nine to thirteen years, are ordered to stay behind to guide

Miss Godwin, the town schoolteacher, in her search for aboriginal paintings which one of the boys said he saw in a cave in a neighboring hill.

A freak cyclonic storm hits the town shortly after the group arrives at the cave, causing heavy damage and completely demolishing the road to Stanley, thereby cutting the children off from their families. By the time their fathers make their way back to Hill's End, the children have organized themselves, not without a few quarrels and misunderstandings, into a working unit and are able to show their elders that the town can be rebuilt.

The unconscious courage shown by the seven and their struggle for survival under the most adverse conditions holds the reader's interest throughout the book. Not one of them is a hero, but each does what he feels called on to do for the good of the others. Each of the children, as a result, is a bit more grown up after the ordeal than before.

Call It Courage, by Armstrong Sperry. New York: Macmillan, 1947. 95p.
    THEME: Boy's self-mastery by overcoming a fear of the sea
    AUDIENCE: Boys and some girls
READING LEVEL: Grade 5   INTEREST LEVEL: Ages 10–13

Mafatu is afraid of the sea. He lives on an island in the Pacific, and the pounding of the surf surrounds him every minute of every day. Overhearing some of the boys laughing at him, at the chief's son who is afraid, Mafatu sets off in a fragile outrigger canoe with a half-dozen green drinking nuts, his fish spear, a dog, and an albatross. He knows he has to prove his courage to himself and the others or he can no longer live in their midst. Facing the dangers of the sea, he conquers his fear of it, and finding himself on an island with the dreaded Eaters-of-Men, he again demonstrates his courage.

Mafatu proves that it is possible to rise above one's fears, to conquer not only nature but self.

Thunder Country, by Armstrong Sperry. New York: Macmillan, 1960. 150p.
    THEME: Boy's meeting the challenge of hostile forces of nature
    AUDIENCE: Boys
READING LEVEL: Grades 5–6   INTEREST LEVEL: Ages 10–15

Rare bird specimens lure Chad Powell and his ornithologist father to the "Thunder Country" of Venezuela, where no white man has ventured before. Thunder Country, home of the sacred quetzal bird, is a country where danger from wild panthers, man-eating *caribes,* and head-shrinking Indians form the background for the disasters that befall the expedition. A surprise occurs when Redskin, a native boy shamed by his people, casts his lot with the group and leads them to the unexplored territory they seek.

The savagery of the jungle, its inhabitants and climate, command the best within Chad and his group. Nature does not outwit them, and they return home with many specimens for study.

The Long Winter, by Laura Ingalls Wilder. New York: Harper, 1953. 335p.
      THEME: Courage and resourcefulness when blizzards strike
      AUDIENCE: Girls, possibly boys
READING LEVEL: Grade 5   INTEREST LEVEL: Ages 9–13
When an old Indian warns Pa Ingalls that it will be a hard winter, Pa moves the family from their Dakota Territory claim into town. Early and frequent blizzards soon prove the Indian to be correct, and before Christmas the little town lies buried in snow, with schools closed and supplies cut off. When the need for food becomes desperate, two young men from the town make a dangerous trip across trackless white prairie to secure wheat, saving the settlers from starvation. It is May before the snows melt sufficiently for the trains to come through, bringing supplies for a belated, but gay, Christmas celebration.

The warm relationships and undaunted spirits of the Ingalls family through trial by continuous blizzards and the bravery of young men who risk their lives to save others, are reassuring evidence of man's courage and resourcefulness in time of trouble. Here are worthy models for young moderns.

The Value of Education
and
the Dropout

Concern for the youth who leaves school without adequate education is widespread, earnest, and sincere. . . . The roots of our concern are in the recognition that educational handicaps make it difficult for the individual to sustain himself with dignity in modern society.

HELEN F. FAUST

Eagle Feather, by Clyde Robert Bulla. New York: Crowell, 1953. 88p.

THEME: Navajo Indian boy's realizing his wish to go to school

AUDIENCE: Boys

READING LEVEL: Grade 3   INTEREST LEVEL: Ages 8–10

Eagle Feather dislikes the idea of school until he visits the trading post with his father, meets a boy his own age, and learns what school would mean to him in companionship and knowledge. Now that he is eager to go, a moment's careless tinkering with Cousin Crook Nose's truck robs him of an immediate chance. He must now pay for damages in service. Unhappily, the greedy cousin does not release him when his term of work expires, so Eagle Feather runs away. Finally, rescued by his father, Eagle Feather is assured that he can now live at home again, and go to school at the same time.

The advantages of formal education are pointed out in this easy-to-read Indian adventure story.

She Wanted to Read, by Ella Kaiser Carruth. Nashville: Abingdon, 1966. 80p.

THEME: Mary Bethune, herself eager to read as a child, devoted her life to the education and advancement of the Negro in America

AUDIENCE: Girls and boys

READING LEVEL: Grades 4–5   INTEREST LEVEL: Ages 9–14

Born of parents who had once been slaves, Mary lived on a South Caro-

The titles in this section originally appeared in "Books as an Aid in Preventing Dropouts," compiled and annotated by the Troubled Child Subcommittee, AHIL, American Library Association, in the February 1969 issue of *Elementary English.*

lina cotton plantation as a child. She spent long hours in the fields, but her fierce determination to learn to read was rewarded when at ten she started school. Scholarships made it possible for her to go on to higher education. Wanting desperately to share her knowledge with others of her race, she opened her own school in Florida. With a determined spirit and the help of philanthropists, Mrs. Bethune finally developed a coeducational college of which she became president. Her work attracted national attention and grew in scope until she became a renowned educator and civic leader.

The story here told is an inspiring testimony to the rich fruits of education to one who early not only "wanted to read," but throughout her later life determined that others would share her knowledge.

Note: Two biographies of Mary Bethune for older readers are:
Mary McLeod Bethune, by Catherine O. Peare. New York: Vanguard, 1951. 219p.
Mary McLeod Bethune, by Emma G. Sterne. New York: Knopf, 1957. 268p.

High School Drop Out, by John Clarke. New York: Doubleday, 1964. 143p.
>   THEME: A boy quits school and realizes his mistake
>   AUDIENCE: Boys
READING LEVEL: Grades 4–5   INTEREST LEVEL: Ages 13–16
Fed up with school, convinced he can do something bigger and better, Joe Bancroft quits. His parents, especially his father, go along with his plans to work and earn good money because their lives have been tuned to work at an early age. Only Joe's girl, Cara, tries to change his mind.

Joe's high hopes soon become depressing rejections and short-term jobs; he tries garage work and peddling fake perfume and cleaning gadgets. When he finds himself involved in handling stolen furs, Joe faces the fact that he's an ill-equipped innocent in a hard world. He returns to school.

This is no fairy tale, but a graphic, credible reflection of what many a boy is thinking and doing. When Joe mutters, "School is nothing but a drag!" many boys will agree; but when he vows after repeated failures, months later: "I'm going to make it," his real-life counterparts may give returning to school a second thought.

Petunia, by Roger Duvoisin. New York: Knopf, 1950. unp.
>   THEME: A silly goose learns the meaning of education
>   AUDIENCE: Boys and girls
READING LEVEL: Grades 2–3   INTEREST LEVEL: Ages 6–9
Petunia, a silly goose, finds a book and thinks that because she owns it,

she is automatically wise. Considering herself an authority on everything, Petunia gives free and incorrect advice to her barnyard friends, making them unhappier than they were before. Not until an explosion which she causes opens the covers of the book does Petunia see the writing inside. She realizes then: "It is not enough to carry wisdom under my wing. I must put it in my heart and in my mind. And to do that I must learn to read." With a new understanding of wisdom, Petunia starts her education.

Petunia's misadventures are hilarious and will amuse the readers, but the message for education and for reading is strong. The book could be used with younger children who do not see the value in learning to read.

Drop-out, by Jeannette Eyerly. Philadelphia: Lippincott, 1963. 189p.
>   THEME: Teen-age boy and girl drop out of high school and try to elope
>   AUDIENCE: Boys and girls
> READING LEVEL: Grades 7–8   INTEREST LEVEL: Ages 12–15

Donnie Muller, a high school senior, and her handsome classmate, Mitch Donaldson, are both faced with unpleasant home situations involving parents who do not understand them or allow them to make decisions on their own. They try to solve these problems by dropping out of high school and eloping to the next city. Afraid of being caught, upon reaching the city they separate and try to get jobs to live on. Both of them find that their lack of high school diplomas automatically puts worthwhile jobs out of reach. When it becomes apparent that their present job opportunities will lead them to a life of frustration and unhappiness, they decide to return home and face the censure of their families to achieve the education necessary to become independent.

The book vividly and realistically pictures the plight of high school dropouts in their search for independence and gainful employment. It points up the necessity of an education for rewarding employment.

Runaway Teen, by Ann Finlayson. Garden City, N.Y.: Doubleday, 1963. 143p.
>   THEME: Teen-age girl runs away from home and school
>   AUDIENCE: Girls
> READING LEVEL: Grades 4–5   INTEREST LEVEL: Ages 12–14

Libby Canfield runs away to Chicago when she feels she is slighted by her mother and stepfather on her sixteenth birthday. Because she lacks a high school diploma, she is able to get only monotonous employment. She rooms with a family of limited means, who all work for the good of the family, but whom she considers dull. For recreation she goes with a local gang, is looked upon as a member of it, and almost gets into serious trouble.

Her eyes open to what she has become and what the gang means by "fun," she makes peace with her family and decides to finish high school.

The book realistically conveys Libby's struggle between the knowledge that she is trapped in her job and her reluctance to return to her parents, a conflict which is only resolved when she sees where her purposeless life is leading her. Her sense of frustration at the monotonous aspect of her job speaks volumes for the value of a high school diploma.

I, Adam, by Jean Fritz. New York: Coward, 1963. 255p.
> THEME: Boy, set on being a farmer, finds his place in the world of words
> AUDIENCE: Boys and girls
READING LEVEL: Grades 6–8   INTEREST LEVEL: Ages 12–14

By the time he graduates from high school in 1850, Adam Crane's education under an insensitive schoolteacher has not been one to encourage him to go further. His ambition is to be a farmer, and, when his father goes on his last whaling voyage, Adam precedes the family to the farm which is to be their home. In the following months, Adam is almost driven to despair by the trickery and irresponsibility of the present owner of the farm and by the farm work itself which, surprisingly, holds no pleasure for him.

In his depression, Adam turns to a neighbor, Pen Jackson, a young schoolteacher whose teaching is so interesting and his enthusiasm for reading so contagious that Adam begins to look forward eagerly to rainy days when he can read his books. By the time his father returns, Adam is ready to admit that he will be happier in the world of words than on a farm.

Adam's reluctance to take up books again and his growing joy in them are realistically portrayed. The story could be used as an example of what books and reading can mean to a boy who, like Adam, was unfortunate in his earlier education.

I Will Try, by Legson Kayira. New York: Doubleday, 1965. 251p.
> THEME: A poor boy determines to receive an education
> AUDIENCE: Boys and girls
READING LEVEL: Grade 8   INTEREST LEVEL: Ages 12 up

Legson Kayira is determined to receive an American education despite his poverty. Even walking from his home in Nyasaland to the coast 2,500 miles away, without a passport or knowledge of whether he could get one, seemed worth the risk. He had no school or friends to come to in America, only a dream. People were kind to him during the long coastward walk and his faith and energy were constantly renewed by this. His impressions of America and his experiences traveling and speaking to groups provide an interesting insight into our country. Legson has returned to his homeland, where he is taking his place as an educated leader in the emerging country of Malawi.

An unforgettable personality and a story to inspire anyone with seemingly impossible problems in acquiring an education.

The Rock and the Willow, by Mildred Lee. New York: Lothrop, 1963. 223p.

> THEME: Family poverty and girl's conflict with severe father who doesn't hold with higher education
> AUDIENCE: Older girls

READING LEVEL: Grade 7   INTEREST LEVEL: Ages 13–18

Growing up on a poor Alabama farm, the oldest girl in her family, Enie has little time for herself. Yet she manages some precious moments alone on a rock under the drooping willow tree, where she enjoys reading and writing in her composition books. Encouraged by a teacher who sees in Enie great potential for writing, Enie dreams of leaving her drab environment and going to college. The story takes her through four years of high school, sees her mature through family illness and death, her first love, and her stern father's remarriage to a woman she resents. Strangely enough, it is this marriage which provides the seemingly impossible chance to go to college.

Written with insight and deep feeling, here is a book to give hope to the aspiring but economically disadvantaged adolescent. The fulfillment of Enie's dream to go to college may stir new hope within the reader to hold fast to her dreams.

That Bad Carlos, by Mina Lewiton. New York: Harper, 1964. 175p.

> THEME: Puerto Rican boy's adjustment to big city life, with its advantages and temptations
> AUDIENCE: Boys, especially those with foreign background

READING LEVEL: Grade 4   INTEREST LEVEL: Ages 9–11

Carlos has a penchant for getting into trouble, although he doesn't intend to be bad. His proneness to be impulsive and easily influenced by friends make his first year in New York City one of repeated difficulties. Making friends with Ricardo, who works in a television and radio repair store, Carlos doesn't realize that the bicycle Ricardo offers to let him ride is "borrowed" without leave. He narrowly escapes involvement with the law, but through an understanding teacher is absolved and led to more responsible behavior.

Readers who are newcomers to a large city may identify with Carlos and Ricardo. They will also see school in a favorable light through the good student-teacher relationships and in Ricardo's decision that to realize his ambition, he must return to school.

The Way of the Wind, by Polly Mark. New York: McKay, 1965. 186p.
  THEME: Difficulties in obtaining an education in Borneo
  AUDIENCE: Girls
READING LEVEL: Grade 7   INTEREST LEVEL: Ages 12 up
  Mari had one dream toward which all her efforts were directed—to obtain an education and teach. Living in present-day Borneo among the traditions of the Iban people, however, she finds her dream predestined to failure. Girls are to remain in the home, help their parents, marry, and establish their own homes. While Mari's parents have allowed her to attend the mission school, they now expect her to give up her schooling and remain with them. A romance with a youthful teacher at the school shows Mari the direction of her future. Hard work and determination to succeed turn obstacles to advantages for her. Her struggle for an education in Borneo will appeal to American teens who have similar problems and dreams.

Pointed Brush, by Patricia Martin. New York: Lothrop, 1959. 29p.
  THEME: Value of education is proved to Chinese father
  AUDIENCE: Boys and girls
READING LEVEL: Grade 3   INTEREST LEVEL: Ages 8–10
  Chung Yee is sad because Father will not allow his five elder brothers to attend school with him. His teacher has told him "that there is power in the written word," and he knows that Father wishes his sons to be powerful and strong. When Elder Uncle is falsely accused of stealing a neighbor's water buffalo and put into a bamboo jail, each of the five elder brothers attempts to free him by physical strength, but each fails. Then Chung Yee writes a letter declaring his uncle's innocence and fastens it to the teahouse wall. The village scholars read the notice and secure Elder Uncle's freedom. When Father learns that Chung Yee's letter has effected Elder Uncle's release, he declares: "All our sons shall go to the teacher. They shall grow wise, knowing the written word."
  Young readers will enjoy the colorful book, and through it may gain new respect for learning.

Carver's George, by Florence Crannell Means. Boston: Houghton, 1952. 176p.
  THEME: A former slave's struggle to get an education, and his
         emergence as a great scientist
  AUDIENCE: Boys and girls
READING LEVEL: Grade 5   INTEREST LEVEL: Ages 9–12
  "He's puny. Don't know if he's worth saving," and the old man put a bundle of rags, the baby of a slave who had been stolen, into Mrs. Carver's hands. She nursed the child, named him George, and watched him grow.

George wasn't strong in much except determination, and that alone led him to school, where he cooked and did laundry and other chores to earn his way. At Tuskegee his research into the uses of the peanut was only one of his contributions to the world, and especially to the small farmer in the South.

The life of George Washington Carver has many things to say to young people today, for he could take the lowliest task and make it worthwhile. "He proved that a black slave baby who had been thrown away could become one of the great men of the world" with the help of an education.

Note: Two biographies of George Carver for older readers are:

Dr. George Washington Carver, by Shirley Graham and George D. Lipscomb. New York: Messner, 1944. 248p.

George Washington Carver, by Rackham Holt. New York: Doubleday, 1943. 342p.

Rookie Quarterback, by Jackson Scholz. New York: Morrow, 1965. 218p.

> THEME: High school football star becomes a dropout before realizing the value of education
>
> AUDIENCE: Boys

READING LEVEL: Grade 6   INTEREST LEVEL: Ages 11–17

Oversized through elementary school, Tim Barlow is just the right size for high school football. Overwhelmed by too much attention and admiration as a sophomore star, Tim neglects his studies and fails several subjects. Ineligible to play and unable to take the jibing of the fans, he becomes discouraged, drops out of school, and joins the Navy. Returning home still interested in football, Tim joins the Cougars, a local sandlot team. With encouragement from the coach Tim gets his high school diploma through correspondence. He is scouted by the Mohawks, a professional club, and learns that many of the players have college degrees and are continuing with further education. An introduction to architecture by a teammate convinces Tim that this is his field. Football becomes a means to an end as Tim becomes a rookie quarterback with a dream.

A book replete with football action and excitement which carries a message for education, even for the dropout.

Annuzza, A Girl of Romania, by Hertha Seuberlich. Chicago: Rand McNally, 1962. 198p.

> THEME: A peasant girl's attempt to "better herself"
>
> AUDIENCE: Girls

READING LEVEL: Grade 7   INTEREST LEVEL: Ages 12–17

While the peasant children in the Carpathian mountain village are content to follow the centuries-old pattern of working in the maize fields,

Annuzza holds onto a dream of leaving home and getting an education. Her father, prone to drink and temper, reminds her, "You're a peasant's daughter, that's what you are, and you're going to stay one too. There'll be no reading and writing here." Only when she composes an essay, "My Dreams," and passes an examination does she find her chance to go to high school in the city. At first Annuzza pretends she is a wealthy landowner's daughter, renouncing her village and her simple parents. After much self-analysis she confesses her deception, admits she will always be a village girl, and returns home to be a teacher.

This honest, mature junior novel is a moving testament to the power of education not merely to lift a person *beyond* his background, but to offer a satisfying role *within* a humble setting.

Roosevelt Grady, by Louisa Shotwell. New York: World, 1963. 151p.
    THEME: Efforts of a boy in migrant family to get an education
    AUDIENCE: Boys and girls
READING LEVEL: Grade 4   INTEREST LEVEL: Ages 9–13

As the truck travels to yet another migrant workers' camp, the children listen to Mother telling their favorite story about her home in "the olden days." But nine-year-old Roosevelt is more interested in the future, and whispers to his mother, "Now let's you and me talk about our secret." Roosevelt's secret dream is for a house where the family can live a long time, in a community where he can "belong" and go to one school long enough to find out about "putting into" in arithmetic. He learns from a friend about Elliot's Bus Camp, where there may be a chance for the family to stay through a year. He and his mother begin to plan and scheme, and when they arrive at the camp, there is promise that they will realize their dream.

The reader will recognize Roosevelt, his family, and the teacher who finally tells him about "putting into" as real people. The boy's eagerness for continuing education is convincing evidence of its importance.

The Far Frontier, by William O. Steele. New York: Harcourt, 1959. 185p.
    THEME: Frontier boy adds book learning to woodcraft
    AUDIENCE: Boys
READING LEVEL: Grade 4–5   INTEREST LEVEL: Ages 9–12

Young Tobe wouldn't mind so much being bound out to Mr. Evans, a frontiersman, or even the blacksmith, but having to work for Asa Twistletree is just too much. Not only is Mr. Twistletree odd-looking, with his spindly legs and thick spectacles, but he spends most of his time watching beetles, wild flowers, or birds. Tobe finds, however, that guiding Mr. Twistletree through wild Tennessee territory is anything but dull. In an encounter with a "woodsy," their only rifle is stolen. Later they discover an interesting old fort where they are captured by the fierce Chickamauga Indians and face torture and possible death. Here Tobe finds that while Mr. Twistletree doesn't know how to make a fire or take care of himself in the woods, he is brave and has much knowledge to share with a boy.

Tobe is challenged by the values he finds in the "letters" Mr. Twistletree teaches. He discovers that knowledge begins with an open mind and a desire to learn and can take place even while he is a captive of the Chickamauga.

Senior Drop-out, by James Summers. Philadelphia: Westminster, 1965. 174p.

      THEME:　High school dropout decides to return to school
      AUDIENCE:　Boys and girls
READING LEVEL:　Grade 7　 INTEREST LEVEL: Ages 12 up

Three years of military school with its stern discipline quiets Lon Renton's love for education. When he is a senior, his father invites him to live with him and his new wife, a kindergarten teacher, and attend their local school. Reluctantly Lon agrees. While he lives in his father's house, he feels isolated from the family. Then he meets Hermine. She brings love into his life and becomes his reason for existence. Desiring to marry her, he quits school and attempts to obtain a job that will make him financially able to fulfill his wish. Two obstacles confront him: lack of a high school diploma and Hermine's refusal to marry him until he finishes his education. Yielding to her wishes and society's demands, Lon returns to graduate with his class.

The conclusion, while face-saving, is acceptable. A realistic approach to a problem of many senior boys.

The Magic Maker, by Joyce Varney. Indianapolis: Bobbs, 1966. 176p.

      THEME:　Necessity of education
      AUDIENCE:　Boys and girls
READING LEVEL:　Grades 4–5　 INTEREST LEVEL: Ages 9–11

"How much trouble can one boy take?" asks Twm Twybach. The ordinary troubles faced by any Welsh boy who dislikes school are compounded by the fact that Twm's superstitious grandmother has taught him that he is half *teg,* or white witch, because of his blond hair, rare in Wales. The blond American exchange teacher must be one too, Twm reasons, and her magic will help solve his tardiness and his family's money problems. His father, however, persuades him that ". . . even the people who believe in *tegs* don't trust them. Magic sounds quick and easy, but God's way is the long, hard way."

The Welsh setting and strange-sounding names will not deter reading of this story, reminiscent of *Tom Sawyer*. Twm's father makes an eloquent plea for schooling to keep the boy from the mines, and an experience in their depths persuades Twm that his father speaks the truth.

The Tiger's Tail, by Nancy Veglahn. New York: Harper, 1964. 211p.

      THEME: Tom Nast's efforts, as boy and man, to use his talents to fight corruption

      AUDIENCE: Boys

READING LEVEL: Grades 6–7   INTEREST LEVEL: Ages 12–18

In the 1850s Tom Nast was a fat little boy from Germany who hated school and was repeatedly the butt of taunting gangs in New York City. Wanting desperately to use his ability to draw instead of "wasting his time" in the classroom, Tom left school and enrolled in the National Academy of Design. He soon turned his power as an artist to caricaturing and, joining the staff of *Harper's Weekly,* he launched a lifetime crusade against the thieving, murdering mob of Tweed's Tammany Hall. Much of the credit for smashing the Tweed ring, which he pictured as a tiger, goes to Tom Nast and his biting cartoons.

This picture of a real-life tough man in a tough city will reach boys who know what it feels like to have a fist in the face or a knife in the ribs. Some will understand how Tom hated school and left. Used in a counseling situation this book would reveal that Tom left one school, true, but he went on to another where he received special training for a special skill.

Sex Education
and
Behavior

Only a fool would tell a teen-ager to stop thinking about sex. . . . They are thinking about sex and will continue to think about it. What they need is sound information so they will know how to think about it.

ANN LANDERS

Moving into Manhood, by W. W. Bauer. New York: Doubleday, 1963. 107p.

    THEME: Guidelines on growing up

    AUDIENCE: Boys

READING LEVEL: Grade 7   INTEREST LEVEL: Ages 12–18

"Getting to be a man . . . is much more than merely growing up sexually. It means growing up emotionally and socially and intellectually." With this beginning the author, a doctor, launches boys into a man's world which is reached by physical and emotional changes and is filled with personal and social responsibilities. In addition to giving a complete background on sexual growth in boys and girls, the author deals with the use of tobacco, alcohol, and drugs, and the pitfalls of borrowing money.

The book is brief, direct, and informal, and has the ring of a man in the know speaking straight facts. As Dr. Bauer summarizes: "This book . . . [is] mainly about sex, and we are not going to be coy or cute about it."

Human Growth: The Story of How Life Begins and Goes on; based on the educational film of the same title, by Lester F. Beck. New York: Harcourt, 1949. 124p.

    THEME: Sex education

    AUDIENCE: Boys and girls

READING LEVEL: Grades 5–6   INTEREST LEVEL: Ages 10–14

A simple, factual presentation with helpful diagrams, this book tells how a baby is conceived, is born, and develops into an adult capable of conceiving another baby. Each chapter is followed by answers to questions asked by children after seeing the film.

The Man That You Marry, by Eleanor Stoker Boll. Philadelphia: Macrae
   Smith, 1963. 189p.
      THEME: Understanding the differences between men and women
      AUDIENCE: Girls
READING LEVEL: Grades 7–8   INTEREST LEVEL: Ages 15 up
The Girl That You Marry, by James Bossard and Eleanor Stoker Boll.
   Philadelphia: Macrae Smith, 1960. 190p.
      THEME: Understanding the differences between men and women
      AUDIENCE: Boys
READING LEVEL: Grades 7–8   INTEREST LEVEL: Ages 15 up
   In these companion books, the authors discuss the physical, psychological, and social differences between girls and boys from childhood on. They explain how these differences are reinforced by society's demands upon young people, and why what may seem to be odd behavior on the part of members of the opposite sex is merely the playing of the role that society expects of them.
   The authors trace development through dating, courtship, engagement, wedding, and married life, showing what to expect from the husband or wife and how to deal with the various problems that arise. These informative and enlightening books could be used as bases for discussion.

It Could Happen to Anyone, by Margaret Maze Craig. New York: Crowell,
   1961. 215p.
      THEME: Affection and intimacy of a nice boy and girl
      AUDIENCE: Girls
READING LEVEL: Grade 6   INTEREST LEVEL: Ages 12–17
   For Jean Chelton it was a moment which shook her life. She "looked at the boy beside her and knew. This was no longer a crush. She loved Andy Decker." She and Andy were normal teen-agers with no disadvantages, no hostilities toward parents, no complexes—just two typical young people doing typical things. But a chance moment of privacy, coupled with the driving force of natural impulses, took them to the brink of fullest intimacy. They pulled back, shocked at what they had almost done, and for a time were disillusioned with each other.
   Completely credible in its rendering of a love affair between a regular guy and a regular girl, this book has double merit as a good teen novel and a nondidactic reminder that "it could happen to anyone."

Growing Up, by Karl de Schweinitz. New York: Macmillan, 1965. 54p.

    THEME: Facts of conception, birth, and growth

    AUDIENCE: Boys and girls

READING LEVEL: Grade 5   INTEREST LEVEL: Ages 7–12

This brief book on procreation in animals and humans is a classic work on sex education for children, notable for its fine balance between practicality and wonderment. The author's word choices and analogies clearly identify and explain (without resort to euphemisms) the ways in which living things perpetuate their species. In describing the birth process, the author uses a vivid four-part sequence of pictures to illustrate his text. In addition to his full, factual presentation, the author carefully steers children away from misconceptions. He explains that human beings are moved to mate by love, while animals are driven by seasonal instincts.

This exceptional book belongs in all young people's hands and in the hands of parents who are explaining life to young children.

Love and the Facts of Life, by Evelyn Millis Duvall. New York: Association Press, 1963. 352p.

    THEME: Sex education and behavior

    AUDIENCE: Boys and girls

READING LEVEL: Grade 10   INTEREST LEVEL: Ages 13–18

This replacement for *Facts of Life* and *Love for Teen-agers* is based upon answers to more than 25,000 questions asked by the readers of the original titles. It includes just about every behavioral situation the teenager has to face and provides factual material as well as a sense of direction. It covers maturation, dating, being in love, and what to do about it. For the modern, sophisticated teen-ager.

Why Wait till Marriage? by Evelyn Millis Duvall. New York: Association Press, 1965. 128p.

    THEME: Noted doctor pleads case for premarital chastity

    AUDIENCE: Boys and girls

READING LEVEL: Grade 8   INTEREST LEVEL: Ages 15 up

Everyone does it—or do they? If you are really in love—why not? Is sexual restraint bad for you? Is pregnancy a possibility? What happens to your reputation? These are only a few questions raised and answered straightforwardly by Dr. Duvall. Always pleading the case for premarital chastity, she takes each argument for premarital relations and knocks it down. The book is sprinkled with quotes and case histories of girls and fellows "in trouble." Examples and statistics from scholarly reports and authorities on sex strengthen her case. She doesn't dodge the issues, nor does she preach or talk down. She just presents the facts as she sees them.

A valuable discussion guide for teen-agers, their parents, and all who work with youth.

A Girl Like Me, by Jeannette Eyerly. Philadelphia: Lippincott, 1966. 180p.
>   THEME: The unwed mother
>   AUDIENCE: Girls

READING LEVEL: Grade 6–7   INTEREST LEVEL: Ages 12–18

Quiet and usually dateless Robin James is overwhelmed when Cass Carter tells her that handsome Randy Griffith wants to take her out. They are to double-date with Cass and her boy friend Brew, but when the night arrives the couples separate, with Randy wanting to park immediately and later attend an unchaperoned party. Other evenings with Randy follow a similar pattern until Robin's parents forbid her to date him again. Upset by the turn of events, Robin learns what might have been her fate when Cass tells her "in seven months there will be a baby."

How Cass faces being an unwed mother is dramatically told. The shock of her classmates, Brew's scorn for her and the situation, the bitterness and hurt of her parents as they force her into a home, plus the strong friendship she has with Robin, are all presented. It is a story with a message that teen-age girls will not forget.

Mr. and Mrs. Bo Jo Jones, by Ann Head. New York: Putnam, 1967. 253p.
>   THEME: Precipitate marriage of teen-agers
>   AUDIENCE: Girls

READING LEVEL: Grade 8   INTEREST LEVEL: Ages 14–18

"I was sixteen, and Bo Jo was seventeen when we got married." Thus begins the first-person story of a marriage of mere babes. From the beginning the reader wants to know July, the narrator, and Bo Jo better, and becomes rapidly interested in their suddenly blighted lives. "We got our kicks from Joan Baez records, J. D. Salinger, pizza, and foreign films." But intimacy and approaching parenthood end these sources of fun, and July and Bo Jo elope into a loveless marriage. The book is the story of their marriage, their accelerated leap into maturity, and the painful confrontation of two social classes represented in the parents who try to manage their lives. The dialogue and the sensitive rendering of young people's hurts and emotional crises rank this novel high among stories about teen-age mothers-to-be.

Love and Sex in Plain Language, by Eric W. Johnson. Philadelphia: Lippincott, 1965. 68p.
>   THEME: Sex, love, and reproduction
>   AUDIENCE: Girls and boys

READING LEVEL: Grade 6   INTEREST LEVEL: Ages 12–17

Clearly and objectively written and using technical terms, this book treats the subjects of sex, love, and reproduction, showing the interrelationship between them, and pointing out the differences between men's and women's reactions to sex. It contains some very sensible, down-to-earth advice for teen-agers about petting, necking, and premature relationships. It also contains explicit diagrams to illustrate the sections of human anatomy, and discusses birth control.

Since the book is so forthright, it could be used as a basis for discussion by teen-agers of their responsibilities and their questions. There is no false modesty or beating around the bush. A very honest book on an important subject.

Ann Landers Talks to Teen-agers about Sex, by Ann Landers. New York: Prentice-Hall, 1963. 131p.

> THEME: Discussion of problems teen-agers express about sex
> AUDIENCE: Boys and girls

READING LEVEL: Grade 7   INTEREST LEVEL: Ages 12 up

In her usual straightforward manner Ann Landers answers letters submitted to her by teen-agers from all over the country. Going steady, the problems involved, and how to break up with a steady are discussed in great detail. Alcohol, venereal disease, homosexuality, and their connection with teen-agers are probed in separate chapters. Ann Landers faces the controversial questions squarely and gives her own opinions. All of her medical facts have been checked by a doctor and are accurate.

Miss Landers has produced a book of sound advice—one which would be very useful for teen-age discussion groups.

Too Bad about the Haines Girl, by Zoa Sherburne. New York: Morrow, 1967. 189p.

> THEME: The problems attendant to pregnancy out of wedlock
> AUDIENCE: Girls

READING LEVEL: Grades 6–7   INTEREST LEVEL: Ages 14–18

Melinda Haines is an attractive high school senior, popular with her classmates and loved by her family. In love with Jeff, her world tumbles down around her when she realizes she is pregnant. Trying to decide how to handle this nightmare situation, she is tempted to have an abortion, but when she tells Jeff of her plans, he tries to dissuade her. Even though it means temporarily giving up his cherished plans to go to college, Jeff suggests marriage. At the last minute, Melinda finds she can't go through with the abortion, and after much anguish, she tells her parents of her pregnancy. The reader is left to assume that Melinda and Jeff will marry and take leave of their carefree youth.

Melinda's anguish over her pregnancy, the distress it will bring to her family, the reversal of plans for the future are made vividly real to the reader, and should give pause for thought. The place of the family in such a dilemma is strongly presented.

It's Time You Knew, by Gladys Denny Shultz. Philadelphia: Lippincott, 1955. 221p.

    THEME: Physical and emotional aspects of growing up
    AUDIENCE: Girls
READING LEVEL: Grade 7   INTEREST LEVEL: Ages 12 up

Written for younger teen girls, the author discusses physical and emotional changes which affect the adolescent at puberty. Social attitudes are related to these changes, and some guidelines for acceptable behavior are suggested without an attempt to moralize. The approach is informal, but the discussion is thorough and accurate. Terms used are explained clearly and honestly.

As with other factual presentations of this type, the book is most effective when presented as part of, or as follow-up to, discussions with a responsible adult.

Letters to Jane, by Gladys Denny Shultz. Philadelphia: Lippincott, 1960, revised edition. 222p.

    THEME: Mother's answers to a daughter's questions about sex
    AUDIENCE: Girls
READING LEVEL: Grade 9   INTEREST LEVEL: Ages 16 up

Jane, a college student, encounters a problem when after a few beers and a few kisses with her boy friend, Tim, she "isn't herself any more." She even wonders, "Will I ever dare to kiss a boy again?" To help ease her mind, she writes to her mother and seeks advice. Her mother answers all her questions frankly. From this letter grows a correspondence that Jane shares with the girls in her dormitory. They ask questions that deal with petting, birth control, virginity, early marriage, and mother-daughter relationships, and "Mrs. L." responds warmly and sincerely.

"Mrs. L." handles the problems that young people face with honesty and rare insight. This book would be excellent for parent–teen-age discussions on dating and sex.

Sex before 20: New Answers for Youth, by Helen Southard. New York: Dutton, 1967. 121p.

    THEME: Answers to questions young people have about sex
    AUDIENCE: Boys and girls
READING LEVEL: Grade 8   INTEREST LEVEL: Ages 16 up

"This is a book about sex but, more important, it is a book about you." Presenting the facts about sex, then proceeding to discuss the role of sex in dating, the author places the important questions squarely in front of the reader. Case histories illustrate various problems encountered in the dating relationship, and a chapter on the generation gap in communication focuses attention on severe problems too often not discussed. Mrs. Southard gives keys to working out problems as they arise.

This is an unusual book, up-to-date in philosophy. It offers the reader a clear idea of sexual freedom and sexual responsibility.

Love, or a Season, by Mary Stolz. New York: Harper, 1964. 260p.
    THEME: Physical attraction vs. friendship
    AUDIENCE: Girls
READING LEVEL: Grade 8   INTEREST LEVEL: Ages 14–16
As he poses for one of Nan's sketches, Harry Lynch discovers that Nan Gunning has become something very special to him. She is radiant and changeable, one minute a child, the next a very desirable young lady, and the two grow more and more aware of each other. Finally on the day after the boat club dance their ardor oversteps social convention, then quickly cools in the face of an astonished and irate Mr. Gunning. Harry is forbidden to see Nan, and in his disturbed state over his pain and humiliation, is involved in a car accident which kills an old man.

Nan and Harry are sensitive young people caught by forces beyond their control. Harry's need for love after the death of his mother and Nan's desire to help him, combined with mutual interest and "chemistry," pull the two close. Their story will appeal to mature, thoughtful young people.

The House of Tomorrow, by Jean Thompson. New York: Harper, 1967. 179p.
    THEME: Unwed mother in Salvation Army home
    AUDIENCE: Girls
READING LEVEL: Grade 7   INTEREST LEVEL: Ages 13–18
Written under a pseudonym, this diary chronicles the story of a twenty-year-old New England college student who has an affair with a married man and becomes pregnant. She does not want to involve him or her own family with her problem, and because her family will be out of the country for a year, she feels she can risk not being discovered. So Jean travels to California and enters a Salvation Army home for unwed mothers. Forced for the first time to think of her future and her new responsibility, she gradually changes from a self-centered individual to one who learns selflessness for her child's sake.

This diary relates Jean's experiences and thoughts while awaiting the birth of her child. It is an honest, straightforward presentation uncluttered by sentimentality. Her story will be invaluable reading for teen-age girls.

Self-Discovery
and
Self-Realization

The gradual development of self is a process of which we are usually unaware. Seeing stages of development in a literary figure may help the child to realize that he, too, is becoming a unique person.

CHARLOTTE HUCK AND DORIS KING

Screwball, by Alberta Armer. New York: World, 1963. 187p.

THEME: Polio victim's difficulty, and final success, in achieving recognition in his area of ability. Rivalry and slight jealousy between twins

AUDIENCE: Boys

READING LEVEL: Grade 5   INTEREST LEVEL: Ages 10–14

Mike acquires the name "Screwball" because he prefers to make things from junk, rather than engage in sports and group activities as does his husky twin, Patrick. Left with muscle weakness after polio in early childhood, Mike is shy and self-conscious, but longs to be like his twin in the ability to make friends and excel in some activity. His chance comes when the family moves from the farm to Detroit, where an understanding truant officer learns of Mike's interest in mechanics. He gives the twins directions for making a soapbox racer, and encourages them to enter racers in the Detroit Derby. Building and skillfully operating a racer absorbs Mike completely for many weeks, and his determination to excel in this effort is rewarded on the speedway.

A story in which the potential for individual achievement and self-respect, within the framework of love and cooperation, is pointed out. Hopefully the reader can come to identify with Mike when he says: "It feels good to know who you are and that it is right to be that person."

The titles in this section originally appeared in "Self-discovery through Books," compiled and annotated by the Troubled Child Subcommittee, AHIL, American Library Association, in the December 1968 issue of *Child Welfare.*

Kep, by Zachary Ball. New York: Holiday, 1961. 207p.

> THEME: Fifteen-year-old boy's struggle to work through guilt, grief, and loneliness to find himself

AUDIENCE: Boys

READING LEVEL: Grade 6   INTEREST LEVEL: Ages 12 up

When Kep Lanning kills his father in a hunting accident, he is left a guilt-ridden, grief-stricken, lonely orphan. The foster home in Mississippi to which he is sent affords every physical comfort but, at first, no acceptance by his foster father. It is in Link Wybel, the town's pariah, that Kep finds real understanding and friendship. Link senses Kep's love for the out-of-doors and his need for the companionship of a pet. He also helps Kep to understand that no problem can be solved by running away from it. Eventually Kep finds the acceptance and love he needs from his foster parents also.

A dramatic and action-packed outdoor story which should have appeal for boys who like animal stories. It also offers many possibilities for identification for boys with problems similar to Kep's.

Benito, by Clyde Robert Bulla. New York: Crowell, 1961. 85p.

> THEME: Boy's learning of independence to attain his ambition in the field of art

AUDIENCE: Boys and girls

READING LEVEL: Grades 3–4   INTEREST LEVEL: Ages 8–12

When Benito, an orphan of twelve, comes to live with Uncle Pedro, he is admonished that he will have much work to do at his new farm home. There will be no time for him to draw pictures with the crayons he brought with him. With Benito's strong urge to draw and carve, this is a severe ultimatum. Later, when selling vegetables for Uncle Pedro in a nearby town, Benito meets a professional artist who encourages his interest, giving him art materials with which to work. Secretly Benito carves the figure of a lady he has once seen, and when it wins professional approval, he has the courage to pursue his dream to learn more and perfect his talent.

An easy-to-read book for boys and girls with an interest in art, or those who need courage to follow a frustrated ambition.

Queenie Peavy, by Robert Burch. New York: Viking, 1966. 159p.

> THEME: Girl's overcoming attitude of rebellion and hostility caused by family problems

AUDIENCE: Girls

READING LEVEL: Grades 5–6   INTEREST LEVEL: Ages 11–13

Thirteen-year-old Queenie Peavy, living in Georgia in the early 1930s, is plagued by her rebellious attitude toward other people. Since her father is in the penitentiary, she is the victim of cruel taunts by her classmates to which she responds with instant anger and hostility. A purposeful tomboy, she resists all efforts by teachers and other interested adults to make her less bristly.

Queenie tells herself that all her troubles are caused by her father's imprisonment for a deed she thinks he did not do. When her father is released, she discovers that he is not the man she dreamed he would be, and that he pays little attention to her. However, she makes a valiant attempt to be on her best behavior so everyone can see that she has turned over a new leaf now that her father is home. When he breaks parole, Queenie almost reverts to her former self; but approval by others of her changed behavior has had its effect. She finds she can face life as it is, instead of as she has wished it to be.

This realistic and moving story of a girl caught by her own actions and attitudes could well provide inspiration for other girls, whose response to unpleasant situations is one of sullenness and rebellion.

Door in the Wall, by Marguerite de Angeli. New York: Doubleday, 1949. 121p.

        THEME: Crippled boy's struggle for self-realization and acceptance
        AUDIENCE: Boys and girls
READING LEVEL: Grades 4–5   INTEREST LEVEL: Ages 9–12

The tolling of the bell awakens Robin to an entirely new world. His parents are off with the King and Queen, the plague has frightened away the servants, and a strange disease holds him a prisoner in bed. He is alone until a kind monk, Brother Luke, takes him to the monastery and helps him to walk again. Later Brother Luke accompanies Robin to the castle of his father's friend, where Robin learns to use his crutches more skillfully, to improve his reading, and to develop an ability with bow and arrow. When the castle is attacked, Robin is able to get help by simply walking away, for who would ever suspect a boy on crutches? Brother Luke has told him that every wall, no matter how high or how long, has a door, and it is the search for his personal door that gives Robin the courage to rescue the besieged castle.

Robin succeeds in proving himself worthy, in spite of being crippled, in a society where physical strength is considered vital.

Two Logs Crossing, by Walter Edmonds. New York: Dodd, 1943. 82p.

        THEME: Teen-age boy's proving himself to be a responsible person
        AUDIENCE: Boys
READING LEVEL: Grades 5–6   INTEREST LEVEL: Ages 10 up

John Haskell, oldest of four children, becomes head of the family upon the death of his father. Knowing that to be accepted by the townspeople, he must overcome his father's reputation for irresponsibility, John works long and hard on the family farm. A local judge interested in John and wishing to test him uses the pretense that John's father owed him $40. Dismayed at the news, John looks to a winter of trapping, which the judge finances, to repay the debt. A successful season turns to disaster when John loses the pelts by not using two logs in crossing a stream as he was advised. Plunged more deeply into debt, John again borrows from the judge and tries another lonely winter in the woods. At last successful, John repays the judge, not only with money, but with the knowledge that he has become an independent, responsible young man.

Set in early America, this brief story of John's coming to respect authority and to prove himself responsible has an important message for modern youth.

Melindy's Medal, by Georgene Faulkner and John Becker. New York: Messner, 1945. 172p.

> THEME: Recognition of young girl as praiseworthy individual by family and self
> AUDIENCE: Girls
> READING LEVEL: Grade 4   INTEREST LEVEL: Ages 9–11

All the men in Melindy's family were recognized for bravery. Gran says it's a shame Melindy is a girl, for she can never win a medal as did her great-grandfather, her grandfather, and her own dear papa. The stories Gran tells about their deeds are the ones Melindy loves best. Still, it *is* too bad that there won't be another treasured medal to add to Gran's box. There is no thought of a medal in Melindy's mind, however, when she discovers a fire in the cloakroom and rushes to the piano to play martial music. Because of her quick action, all the children are saved and Melindy receives the Carnegie Medal for heroism.

The picture of this inner-city family is warm and appealing. Melindy's emergence as a heroine is not unexpected, but will be eminently satisfying to girls too often given tremendous responsibilities and little praise.

A Wild Goose Tale, by Wilson Gage. Cleveland: World, 1961. 112p.

> THEME: Rise to self-confidence of an impulsive, accident-prone boy
> AUDIENCE: Boys, possibly girls
> READING LEVEL: Grades 4–5   INTEREST LEVEL: Ages 9–12

Chuck feels he is probably "the unluckiest boy in the world," for being impulsive and accident-prone he always seems to be in trouble. Then during a week when school is closed, he goes on a camping trip with Uncle

Bill, a nature lover. Chuck learns a lot of nature lore from Uncle Bill, and in identifying with an impulsive goose, also in repeated trouble, Chuck learns something about himself. At the beginning of the trip, Chuck's "jinx" seems to remain, and when he observes, "It would be nice if I could do the right thing once in a while," Uncle Bill replies, "Just keep plugging. . . . The time is bound to come." And it does come when Chuck is able to help Uncle Bill in his effort to get geese to winter on his favorite lake.

Boys will chuckle over Chuck's misadventures, and perhaps achieve a little closer look at themselves as they identify with him. Especially appealing to those with an interest in animal life.

Red Eagle, by Shannon Garst. New York: Hastings House, 1959. 145p.
   THEME: A handicapped Indian boy achieves status
   AUDIENCE: Boys
READING LEVEL: Grades 5–6   INTEREST LEVEL: Ages 10–16
   Lame Foot, a Sioux Indian boy, is named for his deformity. While the other boys of his tribe excel in swimming, wrestling, and mock hunts of the buffalo, Lame Foot is last in the race, weakest in the battle.

As Lame Foot's faith in self falters, old Gray Owl, wise man of the tribe, shows him the way to strengthen his weak muscles and spirit. After many moons Lame Foot succeeds in training a wild horse and in doing the near impossible—capturing a live eagle and its young. Thus Lame Foot earns a new name, Red Eagle.

Any young person with a sense of inferiority may take heart and learn as Red Eagle did that "it is no disgrace to fail. The only disgrace is to stop trying."

I Always Wanted to Be Somebody, by Althea Gibson. New York: Harper, 1958. 176p.
   THEME: A black girl's effort to achieve identity
   AUDIENCE: Girls and boys interested in sports
READING LEVEL: Grade 6   INTEREST LEVEL: Ages 12 up
   Born in Harlem, deliberate truant and pool-hall habituée in her teens, Althea Gibson decided she wanted to make something of her life. Tennis provided her with the means. Learning to play with just a wooden paddle, she progressed to win the Wimbledon and U.S. Lawn Tennis Association championships. She was frustrated by the subtle pressures of prejudice practiced by the fans, other players, and even the black press, but she fought relentlessly to win them over. Getting a foothold in the all-white world of tennis was difficult, but a tremendous triumph for her. After winning the championship, she said, "I've already got the main thing I've always wanted, which is to be somebody, to have identity."

A book to encourage young people to open doors which may seem closed by prejudice or other obstacles.

The Unchosen, by Nan Gilbert. New York: Harper, 1963. 214p.
    THEME: Girls' attempt to win popularity
    AUDIENCE: Girls
READING LEVEL: Grade 6   INTEREST LEVEL: Ages 12–17

Debbie, Kay, and Ellen cling together in their senior year, equally lacking in dates and popularity, equally unchosen. Quite different in tastes, appearances, and home backgrounds, they are alike in their need for boy friends. Ellen, the narrator of the story, pours out her heart to a male pen pal, diets to the point of collapse, and throws an unforgettable party—all as part of the campaign to be "chosen." Ultimately, each girl in her individual way finds her path to friendship with a young man. Each learns that "in the wall are many doors. Be patient, search with diligence, for one will open to your key."

This book bursts its seams with all the exaggerated feelings and yearnings of girls who need admiration and affection. Their experiments in making friends are sometimes comic, often calamitous. Girls will take heart from this book, and will be led to laugh at themselves a bit.

The Year of the Raccoon, by Lee Kingman. Boston: Houghton, 1966.
  246p.
    THEME: The value of a sense of responsibility
    AUDIENCE: Boys and girls
READING LEVEL: Grades 5–6   INTEREST LEVEL: Ages 10–15

Fifteen-year-old Joey is judged by his mother to be a "nice normal average boy," but when he reads these words written by her on a Christmas card each word feels "like a knife wound." Compared to his older brother, who is a talented musician, and his younger brother, who "has great abilities at math and science," Joey feels that he has no talents and that everyone in the family is special except himself. He loves nature and is observant of people, but can't respond to his domineering father's prodding him to decide about his career. A pet raccoon adopted by Joey sparks many family incidents, and eventually helps Joey to mature. At the story's climax, the family doctor points out to Joey that he has one of life's most important attributes in his strong sense of responsibility.

Readers who have trouble finding themselves will readily identify with Joey.

The Rock and the Willow, by Mildred Lee. New York: Lothrop, 1963.
  223p.

THEME: Girl's struggle to "better herself"

AUDIENCE: Girls

READING LEVEL: Grade 5   INTEREST LEVEL: Ages 12–18

For Enie Singleton life stretches monotonously ahead: chores to do, brothers and sisters to tend. Her mother is weary and ailing; her father, stubborn and quick to anger, speaks against schools which will "fill their heads full of nothing, making 'em dissatisfied with what they've got." This is the story of how Enie clings to a dream of college and writing that will take her beyond the sameness, the apathy of her surroundings—an Alabama town during Depression times. Neither the specter of death, the attentions of a jack-of-all-trades man, nor the stubbornness of her father can stifle Enie's dream. As the story ends, she is leaving her home town bound for college, her first step toward becoming a writer.

The message shines through clear and hopeful for all girls: that one need not accept the limitations of environment, that a sense of purpose and unflinching determination can break the cycle of poverty.

Victory over Myself, by Floyd Patterson. New York: Geis, 1962. 244p.

THEME: The rise from delinquent to heavyweight boxing champion

AUDIENCE: Boys

READING LEVEL: Grade 7   INTEREST LEVEL: Ages 12 up

Born in poverty and sensitive to it, Floyd Patterson gave in to the demands of the street and became a delinquent. Arrested for truancy and petty thievery, he was sent to Wiltwyck School for Boys, a haven where he received understanding, a chance to know himself and his abilities, and an introduction to boxing. Boxing became his way out of the asphalt jungle into a life where he was respected as a sports personality. His long years of work, his thoughts as he stood in the ring in triumph and defeat, and his high ideals bring into sharp focus the victory he gained over his environment and himself.

Patterson's story will be particularly encouraging to the reader who needs a second chance.

Jackie Robinson of the Brooklyn Dodgers, by Milton J. Shapiro. New York: Messner, 1957. 190p.

THEME: Curbing of a volatile temper and a black man's acceptance of his responsibility to his race

AUDIENCE: Boys and girls

READING LEVEL: Grade 6   INTEREST LEVEL: Ages 11 up

Jackie Robinson, whose father deserted the family when the boy was but a year old, grew up in the rather poor environment his mother could provide. With encouragement from his mother, he worked his way through college, becoming an all-round athlete before he went into the Army. Upon his discharge from the service he joined a baseball team in the Negro League, where he was singled out to become the first black to play in major league baseball. Jackie rose to the challenge, though not without difficulties, for there was much verbal abuse from grandstand and players, and Jackie was quick-tempered. However, his skillful playing, his successful daring, his deep pride in winning for his team won acceptance for him and for black players who followed him into the majors.

This is not only an absorbing baseball story, but one to demonstrate what determined effort and pride in achievement can add to native ability in the realization of an individual's potential, even when the odds are great.

Ulysses S. Grant, by Henry Thomas. New York: Putnam, 1961. 188p.
>   THEME: Failure in youth does not necessarily continue in adult-
>   hood
>   AUDIENCE: Boys, possibly some girls

READING LEVEL: Grade 6   INTEREST LEVEL: Ages 11 up

Born of undistinguished parents, Ulysses Grant showed little sign of future distinction as a boy. Because he was "pretty good" in arithmetic, his father secured for him a West Point appointment. Here his only achievement was in mathematics and horsemanship, and his classmates looked upon him as the cadet "least likely to succeed." After a brief period of service in the Mexican War, Grant resigned his army commission, looking upon himself as an abject failure. The Civil War brought out his true leadership ability, military genius, and strength of character. As a general he finally covered himself with glory, and won the adulation of many northern Americans. Having gained the people's devotion, he then served two terms as President of the United States.

Young people having trouble finding themselves and lacking in early achievement should find encouragement in Grant's life story.

Banner in the Sky, by James Ramsey Ullman. Philadelphia: Lippincott, 1954. 252p.
>   THEME: Boy's struggle to conquer a forbidding mountain
>   AUDIENCE: Boys and girls

READING LEVEL: Grade 6   INTEREST LEVEL: Ages 11-18

For Rudi Matt, washing dishes and someday managing an Alpine hotel are not the future he wants. There is only one goal in his life—to conquer the Citadel. The great, terrible, solitary pinnacle where sky and mountain meet spelled death for his father fifteen years before. Now Rudi promises himself that he will finish his father's climb. Rudi's vow takes him just a few heartbeats from the top, but the injury of a surly guide from another village forces Rudi to deny himself his victory. He turns back from the peak and takes his companion to safety.

A classic among mountain stories, Rudi's adventure shows how a slight, almost puny boy can become man-sized in courage, self-sacrifice, and achievement.

The Summer I Was Lost, by Phillip Viereck. New York: John Day, 1965. 159p.

THEME: Realization of his abilities by a "constant loser"
AUDIENCE: Boys, possibly girls
READING LEVEL: Grades 5–6   INTEREST LEVEL: Ages 11–15

Paul finds junior high less satisfying than sixth grade, and feels he has no aptitude for leadership or team sports, stressed in his school, nor does he have "power to overwhelm the female sex." The summer after entering junior high he secures farm employment, and soon finds his physical ability unequal to the demands of the job. After a few weeks he is fired, and feels sorry for himself because he has "nothing to be proud of." A camp experience follows, and here Paul becomes lost in mountain wilderness country during a wild storm. When he realizes his predicament, he marshals all his resources to stay alive until rescued, proving to himself and others that he does, after all, have talents and qualities deserving of praise.

Boys lacking in physical stamina and those who have felt lost amid life's struggles will identify with Paul, and they may be encouraged by his story to recognize their own talents and develop them.

The Loner, by Ester Wier. New York: McKay, 1963. 163p.

THEME: A boy's finding of self-worth
AUDIENCE: Boys
READING LEVEL: Grade 5   INTEREST LEVEL: Ages 10–16

A boy without a name lives unloved and loving no one in the rootless pilgrimage of migrant workers from state to state, crop to crop. His loss of an almost-friend, a girl he is just beginning to know, completes his feeling of being a nobody. Collapsed by exhaustion in lonely Montana country, the boy is found by Boss, a sturdy woman who lives alone on the range, having lost her only son. In the growing affection between the boy and grieving mother begins the boy's transition from being nameless to becoming David, the shepherd, from being a loner to becoming someone who is loved and part of a family.

Boys will enjoy David's experiences in a growing awareness of his worth, his adventure in an abandoned mine, and his face-to-face encounter with a bear. They will agree with the deeper message of the book that people need love and a feeling of belonging.

Shadow of a Bull, by Maia Wojciechowska. New York: Atheneum, 1965. 155p.

> THEME: Boy's conflict caused by pressure to follow in his father's footsteps
>
> AUDIENCE: Boys

READING LEVEL: Grade 6   INTEREST LEVEL: Ages 11–14

Manolo Olivar, only son of a famous bullfighter, lives in the shadow of his dead father's image. All who knew his father assume Manolo will be a great fighter like his father and will face his first bull when he is twelve. As the date approaches, Manolo becomes aware that he lacks the necessary love of bullfighting, and, while watching a doctor at work, he discovers that he would rather cure as a doctor than kill as a matador. His best friend's brother, Juan, on the other hand, desperately wants to be a matador but, having no money or influence, is unable to break into the field. When the great day comes, Manolo makes the decision to be true to himself and lets Juan finish the bull.

Manolo's sense of responsibility to his father's friends and his knowledge that he will not be a bullfighter like his father are in constant conflict with each other. Manolo sees no escape from the fate that well-meaning but unseeing adults have made for him. Only in being true to himself does he find the way clear to become a free individual.

They Loved to Laugh, by Kathryn Worth. Garden City, N.Y.: Doubleday, 1942. 269p.

> THEME: Shy girl's learning to hold her own in a boisterous, teasing family
>
> AUDIENCE: Girls

READING LEVEL: Grades 6–7   INTEREST LEVEL: Ages 12–15

When sixteen-year-old Martitia Howland is orphaned by a typhoid epidemic in the 1830s in North Carolina, she is taken in by Dr. David Gardner to live with his family of five boisterous young men and a sober daughter. Martitia, unaccustomed to housework and unused to teasing, finds life very difficult in this industrious and fun-loving household. The daughter, Ruth, shames her into learning to work with her hands, and the affection of the boys gives her the security to laugh. When faced with a choice between staying with this warm but poor family or going to live with her rich but cold aunt and uncle, Martitia chooses the Gardners and is eventually adopted into the family. In a few years, Martitia is a fun-loving, capable person, able to take care of herself and beloved by all in the household.

Martitia's slow but steady progress from a timid and lonely girl to a confident and outgoing young lady would be encouraging to other girls who feel themselves left out of much of the fun of living. A romance between Martitia and the oldest son will add interest for many girls.

Crow Boy, by Taro Yashima. New York: Viking, 1955. 37p.

> THEME: A shy boy's compensation for lack in one talent by achievement in another
> AUDIENCE: Boys and girls

READING LEVEL: Grade 3   INTEREST LEVEL: Ages 7–10

Young Chibi is shy and forlorn as he sits with his classmates day after day in the village school. He is regular in attendance, but because he has trouble learning in school, his classmates call him stupid. Then a friendly new teacher recognizes that although Chibi has difficulty with school subjects, he has other knowledge, skills, and merits. When at the talent show the boy imitates to perfection all kinds of crows, and is honored for six years of perfect school attendance, the derisive name "Chibi" is changed to Crow Boy, and all say: "Yes, he is wonderful."

A short, simple, well-illustrated picture book, deep with meaning. Especially suitable for children lacking academic abilities, but having other skills and accomplishments.

Gangs and Youth
Involved
with the Law

The important contribution of this book list is that it contains books with a FRAME OF REFERENCE for the delinquent or delinquent prone youth . . . Only through empathy or placing themselves in the psychological shoes of others can [delinquents] secure a sincere feeling for their fellow men. The books on this list will provide the opportunity of experiencing empathy with the characters described.

DR. PRESTON SHARP

Durango Street, by Frank Bonham. New York: Dutton, 1965. 187p.
    THEME: Parolee's difficulty in avoiding repeated trouble in an area
            dominated by fighting gangs
    AUDIENCE: Boys
READING LEVEL: Grades 6–7   INTEREST LEVEL: Ages 12–18

Rufus Henry, recently released parolee from Pine Valley Honor Camp, is faced with a dilemma. Almost immediately after his return home, he is attacked by the Gassers, a fighting gang in the neighborhood of the Durango Housing Project. Although it is against parole regulations, Rufus feels he must join another gang to stay alive. Before long he is not only a member of the Moors, but has taken over the leadership. Gang warfare, deceit, thievery, drunkenness, and encounters with police are common experiences of the Moors, even after Alex Robbins, a social worker, associates himself with the gang. Alex's work with the boys brings no magical results, but gradually and often unobtrusively he guides them into more positive avenues of activity. The story ends on a hopeful note, with the likelihood that Rufus will return to school.

That Rufus secretly admires a professional football player whom he believes to be his father may add interest and value for some readers. Readers

---

The titles in this section (except for *The Outsiders* by Susan E. Hinton) originally appeared in "Without Whip or Rod," compiled and annotated by the Troubled Child Subcommittee, AHIL, American Library Association, in the December 1966 issue of *Federal Probation Quarterly.*

with gang experience may glimpse an "out" from their lives of violence and possible death from enemy gangs, and they may note that relating to a social worker can be helpful.

Heartbreak Street, by Dorothy Butters. Philadelphia: Macrae Smith, 1958. 191p.

> THEME: Living in a poor neighborhood
> AUDIENCE: Girls
> READING LEVEL: Grades 7–8   INTEREST LEVEL: Ages 12–15

Kitty Boscz is determined to move herself and her family from her slum neighborhood, where her older brother, Tomas, is being drawn into a gang and her younger brother, Danny, is constantly harried by the local bully. After graduation from high school Kitty takes a factory job to earn money for the move. At the same time she consistently ignores the recreation director's efforts to provide more wholesome activities for teen-agers in the area. When Danny is severely beaten by a member of Tomas's gang, Kitty, her family, and the neighbors realize the menace of the gang to the neighborhood, and begin work to improve conditions. Kitty grows to understand that her attitudes toward her surroundings are more important than the environment itself.

The Boszcs and their neighbors are examples of how people in a neighborhood can drift into acceptance of gangs and their activities instead of taking active steps to divert the boys' energies into more useful channels. There are insight and an honest handling of neighborhood problems here for parents and youth.

The Twenty-third Street Crusaders, by John F. Carson. New York: Farrar, 1958. 183p.

> THEME: Teen-age delinquents on probation
> AUDIENCE: Boys
> READING LEVEL: Grades 6–7   INTEREST LEVEL: Ages 12–16

The seven boys who make up the Twenty-third Street Crusaders are known as a gang of troublemakers. When they disturb the peace in the drugstore one day, the proprietor draws a gun on them. The boys jump him, beating him up. Placed on a year's probation, Joey Gibbs and his buddies seem headed for more serious trouble when a stranger comes into their lives. Ed Sorrell sees their restless indirection and converts them into a winning basketball team.

Valuable as a basketball story with graphic sequences, and as a fictional study of a despairing adult and crime-bent youth. Not without repeated crises and flare-ups of aggression, the gang members and their leader solve their personal problems through teamwork and selflessness. Easy-to-read story in teen-age vernacular.

Drop-out, by Jeannette Eyerly. Philadelphia: Lippincott, 1963. 189p.

> THEME: The difficulties dropouts face when trying to assume adult responsibilities
>
> AUDIENCE: Girls and boys

READING LEVEL: Grade 8 INTEREST LEVEL: Ages 13–18

Donnie, whose stepmother is overly strict with her, and Mitch, whose parents are pushing him, are unhappy high school seniors. When Mitch is offered a good mechanic's job by a flashy stranger who seems to take a personal interest in him, they decide to elope. Their car breaks down before they can reach the job, and their unsuccessful attempts to find work cause them to re-evaluate their goals and their love for each other. When they read in the newspaper that their "benefactor" is the head of an auto theft ring and that one of Mitch's friends was caught with him, they realize how close they have come to ruining their lives. They decide that, even though they are unhappy at home, it is important for them to stay there.

Among the points made in the book are the relative values of short-range and long-range goals and the necessity of having to put up with an unpleasant family life to achieve the education that will allow one to earn an honest living.

Hot Rod, by Henry G. Felsen. New York: Dutton, 1950. 188p.

> THEME: Teen-agers' love of speeding and hostile attitude toward authority
>
> AUDIENCE: Boys and girls

READING LEVEL: Grades 6–7 INTEREST LEVEL: Ages 11–16

Bud's hot rod and his fast, risky driving have earned him the adulation of his peers. He breaks traffic rules and is put on probation with the understanding that he will test his skills in a roadeo against those of a new driver who has respect for others and for authority. Bud loses because of his attitudes and is forced to reassess his belief in speed when, following his example, two small boys and a number of his friends are killed in crashes.

The realistic portrayal of teen-agers at the wheel, their love of speeding, and their defiance of authority add validity to a story which probes one's responsibilities to others and the far-reaching effects of one's actions.

Runaway Teen, by Ann Finlayson. Garden City, N.Y.: Doubleday, 1963. 143p.

> THEME: Resentment over mother's remarriage; inadvertent involvement with a gang
>
> AUDIENCE: Girls

READING LEVEL: Grades 4–5 INTEREST LEVEL: Ages 11–16

Libby Canfield, resentful of her mother's remarriage, is jealous of her stepfather. On an impulse of the moment when she feels neglected on her sixteenth birthday, Libby decides to quit school, run away to Chicago, and become independent. She soon finds that jobs are scarce for those without a high school education, and is forced to take monotonous factory work. For excitement she makes friends with a corner drugstore gang near her boarding house. The friendly interest of her landlady's family saves her from becoming seriously involved with the gang, which is given to violence and thieving. Eventually Libby recognizes her mistakes and returns home.

The story points up how, through resentments and lack of understanding, a teen-ager can become involved with gangs and unsavory activity. The importance of education is also brought out.

Ellen and the Gang, by Frieda Friedman. New York: Morrow, 1963. 191p.
THEME: Preteen girl becomes dupe of older teen-age lawbreakers
AUDIENCE: Girls
READING LEVEL: Grade 5   INTEREST LEVEL: Ages 10–14

Feeling inferior to her talented brother and sister and interpreting her parents' praise of them as a rejection of herself, Ellen seeks approval of older, sophisticated, "forbidden" teen-agers who take advantage of her naiveté and good reputation to cover up their petty thefts. Ellen is shocked and shamed when she discovers she has been duped and momentarily retreats from the world. Constructive entanglement in a recreation program points up her capabilities and restores her self-respect.

The support of Ellen's parents after her near-arrest is significant. Because Ellen's misinterpretations of family, self, and peers are human and characteristic of her age, readers will easily identify with her. Despite simple and pat solutions to problems, the presentation of temptation is realistically drawn. Appropriate for younger and poor readers.

Youth and the FBI, by John J. Floherty and Mike McGrady. Philadelphia: Lippincott, 1960. 159p.
THEME: Nationwide juvenile delinquency and crime
AUDIENCE: Boys
READING LEVEL: Grades 7–8   INTEREST LEVEL: Ages 12–18

An Italian sport car tempts Buck Robbins. He "borrows" it for a few hours and spins off to Connecticut to see his girl. This, Buck's first crime, serves as a catapult into knowledge of FBI methods. He tours the Department of Justice, sees how scientific sleuthing enters into the detection and apprehension of criminals, and how law-enforcement agencies work to prevent juvenile crime. Returning to New York, Buck witnesses a gang rumble quelled by the police.

Buttressed by true cases and statistics on teen-age offenders, this book is never preachy, and achieves the author's theme: "Show any kid the power behind the law and he'll think twice before breaking it."

North Town, by Lorenz Graham. New York: Crowell, 1965. 220p.
   THEME: Adjustment of a southern black to life in a northern city
   AUDIENCE: Boys
READING LEVEL: Grades 6–7   INTEREST LEVEL: Ages 12–18
   David Williams, fresh from racial trouble in the South, tries to adjust to life in an integrated school in the North. Uncertain as to how to treat white boys and how to respond to them, he falls in with a group of black boys who are in trouble with the law. In his desire to become a member of this group, he inadvertently takes a ride with them in a stolen car. His subsequent arrest and its effect on his parents force him to re-evaluate his feelings about his other classmates. Slowly but surely, David comes to realize that he can accept people for what they are without reference to color, and can be accepted by others on the same basis.
   A book to give insight into problems of adjustment to new experiences and environment, and into the ease with which a teen-ager can become involved with the law if he does not stop to think things through and really know his associates.

Knockout, by Philip Harkins. New York: Holiday, 1950. 242p.
   THEME: Achieving identity without joining a gang
   AUDIENCE: Boys
READING LEVEL: Grades 6–7   INTEREST LEVEL: Ages 11–15
   Ted Brett, slightly built and studious, is bullied by his older brother and constantly set upon by the local gang, led by Bud Sturm. After a beating by the gang, he is rescued by Officer Mulligan, who advises him to take boxing lessons at the local PAL unit. Instead, Ted joins a boxing class at the local recreation center, where he proves himself an apt pupil. When Bud and his gang come to the center to challenge him, Ted wins the impromptu match. Upset by his defeat, Bud now takes boxing lessons at the local PAL unit. Both boys enter the Golden Gloves contest and Ted finally defeats Bud once and for all, and henceforth can hold his own against all comers.
   Ted's story is an example of the various avenues open to boys searching for identity, yet unwilling to join gangs whose activities they dislike.

Catch a Brass Canary, by Donna Hill. Philadelphia: Lippincott, 1964. 224p.
   THEME: Teen-ager's rehabilitation through work in a library
   AUDIENCE: Boys and girls
READING LEVEL: Grades 9–10   INTEREST LEVEL: Ages 14–18

Miguel Campos is released from The Institution and returns to his dingy, drab flat in Manhattan's Upper West Side. Trying to cast off his past as a "dumb punk kid," Miguel succeeds in getting a part-time job at the Amsterdam Public Library. At first he meets hostility and suspicion there because of his Puerto Rican background and his police record. The treacherous tentacles of his old gang reach into his life again when he is reminded, "Snake Eye's boys can never chicken out." But these threats and a severe beating do not alter his decision to go straight.

Miguel's library work, his encounters with the gang, and his final renunciation of Snake Eye offer authentic dialogue and depict convincing rehabilitation.

The Outsiders, by Susan E. Hinton. New York: Viking, 1967. 188p.

   THEME: Facing the harsh realities of life in a big city
   AUDIENCE: Boys and girls
READING LEVEL: Grades 6–7   INTEREST LEVEL: Ages 12 up

"Outside" is the East Side, home of the Greasers, long-haired, tough, and poor—hating West Side society kids with their madras jackets and Mustangs. Ponyboy Curtis is one of the Greasers, the youngest member of the gang and proud of his long hair, but different because he watches sunsets, reads, and makes good grades. Ponyboy aches for a world where he won't have to watch rich kids while his brother has to give up college so the family won't be split up. And it is Ponyboy who stands off a gang of West Siders, and holds his best friend Johnny when he dies. "Sixteen years on the streets and you can learn a lot. But all the wrong things, not the things you want to learn," says Pony.

Written by a seventeen-year-old who has seen some of these wrong things, *The Outsiders* is real and alive and grim and touching and *today!*

Pickpocket Run, by Annabel and Edgar Johnson. New York: Harper, 1961. 185p.

   THEME: A restless teen-ager tempted by crime
   AUDIENCE: Boys and girls
READING LEVEL: Grade 7   INTEREST LEVEL: Ages 12–18

Resentful, "prickly as a bur," Dix must choose between the lenient ethics of his Pop, who will do almost anything to make a buck, the easy money of the local sharpy Keno, who plans a motel robbery, and hard, honest work. Driven by his own sullen attitudes, by dishonest values at home, by law-breaking impulses in his peers, and by his need to be independent, Dix approaches crime. In a tense conclusion, he makes his decision, foils the robbery, and sets his goals straight.

This slangy, realistic, hard-hitting story offers a credible dilemma and an optimistic conclusion.

That Bad Carlos, by Mina Lewiton. New York: Harper, 1964. 175p.
> THEME: Puerto Rican boy's adjustment to New York City life, with its advantages and temptations
> AUDIENCE: Boys, especially those with foreign backgrounds
> READING LEVEL: Grades 4–5   INTEREST LEVEL: Ages 9–12

Ten-year-old Carlos and his Puerto Rican family are newcomers to New York City, where Carlos finds much to fascinate him. His proneness to be impulsive and easily influenced by friends, and his great desire to ride a bicycle, soon have Carlos in repeated trouble. When it is discovered that he's been riding a stolen bicycle (innocently), his family and an understanding teacher prevent more serious involvement with the law, and help Carlos to understand the importance of responsible behavior.

Newcomers to any large city may identify with Carlos, and possibly be led by the easily read story to see the wisdom of responsible behavior and the value of continuing education.

Killer, by Richard Parker. Garden City, N.Y.: Doubleday, 1964. 201p.
> THEME: Escape of delinquent boys from an institution
> AUDIENCE: Boys
> READING LEVEL: Grades 10–11   INTEREST LEVEL: Ages 14–18

Mungilla is an institution in Tasmania for "lost but not black sheep" teen-agers who live and work together until they are ready to return to society. McKay, the warden, directs the boys with easy intuition. The scene shifts from relaxed discipline to brooding violence with the arrival of two people: Brec, an insecure martinet serving as substitute warden during McKay's vacation, and Butts, a sadistic young killer. The battle of will and wits between these two quickly engulfs the other boys and leads to a mass escape. Tension mounts as each escaping boy must face the physical hardships of wild terrain and must follow either Butts's brutal lawlessness or his own emerging conscience.

Tough boys and tough talk make a harsh yet hopeful story.

Edge of Violence, by Dorris Riter. New York: McKay, 1964. 245p.
> THEME: Adjustment of a teen-age boy on probation
> AUDIENCE: Boys and girls
> READING LEVEL: Grades 7–8   INTEREST LEVEL: Ages 12–18

Released on probation into the custody of a lawyer living on a ranch,

Dirk Lander leaves Juvenile Hall filled with guilty memories and trepidation. Behind him is an arrest on charges of larceny. Ahead lies—who knows? "He was 17 and he felt his life was over." In the new environment Dirk begins to unwind and to trace the source of his sullen antagonisms and loneliness. Contributing to his adjustment are his affection for his guardian's daughter and his interests in riding and painting.

Dirk's growing self-understanding is credibly told, with realistic lapses into old attitudes and temptations a part of his gradual progress. Readers will appreciate the magnitude of Dirk's decision to reject his former gang members when they force him at gunpoint to drive a getaway car. They will also sense that rehabilitation is possible.

Chip on His Shoulder, by Jo Sykes. New York: Funk & Wagnalls, 1961. 186p.

> THEME: Teen-ager's adjustment from delinquency to "going straight" and from urban to rural environment
> AUDIENCE: Boys
> READING LEVEL: Grades 6–7   INTEREST LEVEL: Ages 12–16

Caught in a rumble with a gun in his belt, sixteen-year-old Hamilton Roark of the Red Whistlers is given a second chance. He takes his chip on his shoulder, his distrust, and his self-doubt to a small Montana town where the Stuart family is willing to take him in. Soon he is moved to reappraise his distrust of people by the kindness of the Stuarts, and he relaxes a little under the influence of mountain views and fresh air. In the outlaw gelding, Chip, he sees the counterpart of his own defiance and loneliness. In healthy, sun-bronzed Billy Stuart he witnesses the kind of self-reliant person he would like to be.

Combined as it is with engrossing details on horse training and handling, Roark's story—his gradual softening into a social being—is entirely convincing.

The Winning Quarterback, by Charles S. Verral. New York: Crowell, 1960. 248p.

> THEME: The far-reaching effects of gang membership
> AUDIENCE: Boys
> READING LEVEL: Grades 5–6   INTEREST LEVEL: Ages 11–14

Pierre "Frenchy" Beaumont, a senior with a good chance of becoming an all-star quarterback, is forced to accept André, his cousin, who is in trouble for his gang activities and is hostile to Frenchy's overtures of friendship. Frenchy catches André in some questionable money-making activities and forces him to a showdown. André confesses that he is being blackmailed by the leader of his gang and is trying to solve his problems by running away. Mrs. Beaumont takes André, against his wishes, to the local police where the situation is clarified and André learns that the law can mean protection as well as punishment.

Realistically, André does not reform completely, but the book ends on a note of hope for him and for his relationships with his peers. The book points out the far-reaching effects of gang participation even after formal ties are broken, and the protective aspects of law-enforcement agencies.

Index to Books for the Troubled Child and Adolescent

18-300

DATE DUE

DEC 1 4 1990		
DEC 0 6 2001		
12/11/01		

30 505 JOSTEN'S